MEN AND THOUGHT IN ANCIENT INDIA

Men And Thought In Ancient India

Radha Kumud Mookerji

MOTILAL BANARSIDASS PUBLISHERS
PRIVATE LIMITED • DELHI

First Edition: Delhi, 1924
Second Edition: Delhi, 1957
Third Edition: Delhi, 1970
Reprint: Delhi, 1996

ISBN: 81-208-1171-2

Also available at:

MOTILAL BANARSIDASS
41 U.A. Bungalow Road, Jawahar Nagar, Delhi 110 007
120 Royapettah High Road, Mylapore, Madras 600 004
16 St. Mark's Road, Bangalore 560 001
8 Camac Street, Calcutta 700 017
Ashok Rajpath, Patna 800 004
Chowk, Varanasi 221 001

PRINTED IN INDIA
BY JAINENDRA PRAKASH JAIN AT SHRI JAINENDRA PRESS,
A-45 NARAINA, PHASE I, NEW DELHI 110 028 AND
PUBLISHED BY NARENDRA PRAKASH JAIN FOR
MOTILAL BANARSIDASS PUBLISHERS PRIVATE
LIMITED, BUNGALOW ROAD, DELHI 110 007

TO

THE REVERED MEMORY OF MY FATHER,

GOPALCHANDRA MOOKERJI, M.A., B.L.,

HIGH COURT VAKIL, BERHAMPORE, BENGAL,

WHOSE SCHOLARSHIP AND INTEREST IN HISTORY

HAVE BEEN A CONSTANT INSPIRATION

(1845--1894)

PREFACE

In this book an attempt is made to present a view of ancient Indian Culture and Civilisation, as seen in some of their best representatives. This method of historical presentation has some special points to recommend it. It gives a reality and concreteness to what may appear to be the somewhat shadowy and abstract ideals of Indian thought, which are, however, very well grasped and visualised when traced in the lives that realise and illustrate them, and even result from them. The history of the world may be well studied as the biography of its Representative Men. These incarnate the history they create.

The history of Hindu India is very well represented in the characters brought together here. Each of them presents an aspect of Indian Thought and Life. Yājñavalkya is the typical and the most historical example of Vedic thought, the fountain-head, and, perhaps, the high watermark, too, of the entire stream of Indian thought. As the outstanding figure of a highly intellectual age, to which humanity owes some of its best literary treasures, and as the chief exponent of the saving knowledge of the Upaniṣads, Yājñavalkya takes his rank as the father of Hindu Philosophy. The next character brought forward is the Buddha, who, born a prince, and a prince among men, lived to achieve the highest enlightenment in the solitude of the forests which produced the wisdom of the Āraṇyakas and Upaniṣads, and discovered a new world of Truth and Love, which well-nigh completed the circle of Indian thought and even extended it over a large part of mankind. Brahmanism and Buddhism are, indeed, the two poles of the world of Indian thought, within which it has been revolving in its orbit through the ages, though they are not to be regarded as poles apart in their contents. The popular view shows sound philosophical judgment in counting the Buddha as one of the Ten Hindu Avatāras.

Asoka stands out as the singular example of a monarch and a man of affairs, proving the best of idealists, who proceeded boldly to organise an empire upon the principle of Right and not of Might, the first, and, perhaps, the only man in the world who proclaimed war as an evil, and believed only in moral conquest, in force of law and not the law of force, Soldiers of his faith invaded the countries on his borders, and beyond, in parts of Europe and Africa, to deliver his message of peace and social service. At home, a Ministry took care of the aborigines and backward peoples, while leaving them politically free. The emperor preferred to be their trustee and guardian. This saving on military expenditure he devoted to the .moral development of his people upon the basis of certain standard ideals and virtues acceptable to all creeds, nay, to all mankind. Thus his empire was the outshaping of Indian Thought at its best, in its widest range and synthesis. One might see in it the world that India would shape, if it were left to her. But, unfortunately, Asoka was too far ahead of his age and even of his posterity, too. An ideal empire founded on the basis of Universal Peace could not stand the shock and collision of historic forces. The ascent of Man has ever been a blind and bloody struggle!

Samudragupta comes next as the Indian type of militarism, who conquered only to liberate, but who stood boldly for the traditional Kṣatriya ideal for a king, that he must extend his authority up to the limits of his country, so that it may attain a political unification under the 'umbrella' of one paramount sovereign.

Lastly comes Harṣa, in whom we find some of the attributes of both Samudragupta and Asoka. Great in War and greater in Peace, Harsa has touched certain heights of greatness rarely equalled in the annals of kingship. His liberality beats all record, while he helped his country after a long interval of time to recover the unity of its history lost in local annals or interrupted by foreign interference.

I owe my special acknowledgments to Dr. F. W. Thomas, M.A., PH.D., the learned Librarian of the India Office, for his kind interest in my work and correction of its proofs.

The system of transliteration adopted here may be indicated by the following examples: *Kṛiṣṇa*, *Lichchhavi*, *Māhavaṃsa*, and *Aṅga*.

RADHA KUMUD MOOKERJI.

UNIVERSITY OF LUCKNOW,
April, 1924.

PREFACE TO THE SECOND EDITION

I am thankful to Messrs. Hind Kitabs Ltd. of Bombay for bringing out the second edition of the work in response to a persistent demand, and also to Messrs. Macmillan and Co. of London for waiving their copyright in favour of this publication.

I regret that my work in Parliament did not leave me the time needed for revising the book, but I may say that the need for such revision was not very imperative, in view of the fact that the work is based on material that is old and fixed, and has been hardly changed by fresh discoveries, literary or archaeological. Only one important addition has been called for, and inserted at the end, on account of the few Inscriptions of Asoka discovered since the first edition.

RADHA KUMUD MOOKERJEE.

January 1957.

CONTENTS

MAPS AND ILLUSTRATIONS

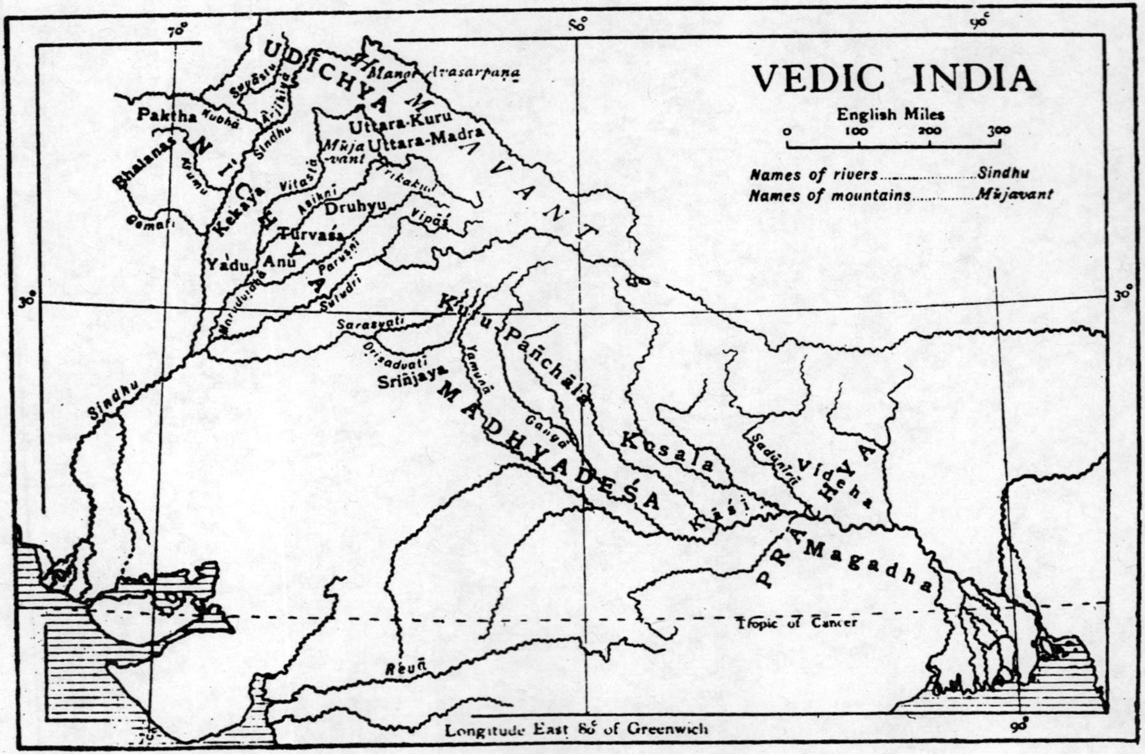
VEDIC INDIA
English Miles
0 100 200 300
Names of rivers .... Sindhu
Names of mountains .... Mūjavant
UDĪCHYA
HIMAVANT
Manor Avasarpaṇa
Uttara-Kuru
Uttara-Madra
Mūjavant
Paktha
Bhalanas
Kubhā
Krumu
Gomatī
Sindhu
Kekaya
Vitastā
Asiknī
Druhyu
Turvaśa
Yadu
Anu
Paruṣṇī
Vipāś
Śutudrī
Marudvṛdhā
Sarasvatī
Dṛṣadvatī
Sṛiñjaya
Kuru-Pañchāla
Yamunā
Gaṅgā
MADHYADEŚA
Kosala
Kāśī
Videha
Sadānīrā
Magadha
Reuñ
Tropic of Cancer
Longitude East 80° of Greenwich
70°
80°
90°
30°

YAJÑAVALKYA

The history of India belies her geography. Mountain-guarded and sea-girt in the north and in the south, India is sharply distinguished from the rest of the world as an indisputable geographical unit. Yet her splendid physical isolation has not been able to shut out foreign influences upon her history. Indeed, nearly all the principal movements of thought in human history have invariably touched India too and left some marks upon her culture or civilisation so as to render it a highly complex and synthetic system. Persian, Greek, Roman, Scythian, Yueh-chi, Hun, Mahomedan and European have all contributed diverse elements to the making of that remarkable composite called the Indian Civilisation ; but the basis of that civilisation was that given by the Indo-Aryan, and that basis has continued through all changes and amid its different phases.

The foundations of Indian Civilisation were fixed roughly during the period 2000-1000 B.C., when the Indo-Aryans began and nearly completed their work of colonising and civilising the Indian continent. which was called *Bhārata-*

varsa, after the name of one of the representative peoples, the Bharatas. This primary and formative phase of Indian Civilisation is represented in the institutions and literature of the Indo-Aryans, and is conveniently designated and distinguished as Vedic Civilisation with reference to its sources in the vast body of Vedic Literature, comprising in the main the three classes of works, the Saṃhitās, Brāhmaṇas and Upaniṣads.

Vedic Civilisation had been the work of numerous sages, or ṛiṣis, and kings, in whom were embodied its characteristic ideals of thought and life. But, unfortunately, most of them are mere names to us, and are almost like mythical personages, concerning whom we can hardly get at any historical facts or biographical details from the records available. The religious history of the Vedic period is associated with many a generation of seers, or ṛiṣis, such as Atri, Aṅgiras, Priyamedha, Bhṛigu, Vasiṣṭha and Viśvāmitra, who produced, and handed down from sire to son, special bodies of Ṛigvedic hymns, which became the property of their respective families; while the political history of the period is represented in the exploits of kings like Sudās, who achieved his great victory over a powerful coalition of ten kings such as Druhyu, Pūru, Anu and the like, who were further supported by their many allied peoples, like the Matsyas, Pakthas, Bhalānas, etc. But, unfortunately, none of these numerous names of the leaders of thought and action in old Vedic society can be given a historic reality for want of concrete details and evidence regarding their life and work, and they must necessarily remain as mere names and abstractions.

There is, however, at least one Vedic character of whom it is possible to work out a comparatively concrete account. Yājñavalkya was a representative man of his age, one of the most typical embodiments of all that was best and highest in Vedic culture and civilisation. He was also one of the last Vedic riṣis, associated with the later developments of Vedic thought and life, as expressed in the elaborate literature of the Brāhamaṇas and Upaniṣads. Hence Vedic culture in its most developed and typical form can be best studied in him, the acknowledged intellectual and spiritual leader of his times.

Yājñavalkya is the first reputed author of the White Yajur-Veda. He is represented as a prominent authority on rituals in the Śatapatha Brāhmaṇa and on philosophy in the Bṛihadāraṇyaka Upaniṣad. Most probably he belonged to the eastern parts of India, because the books associated with him mention only the peoples settled in those parts, such as the Kuru-Pañchālas, Kosala-Videhas, Śviknas and Sṛiñjayas. The same conclusion is indicated by the intimacy of his connexion with the two famous Kuru-Pañchāla Brāhaman scholars, Uddālaka and his son Śvetaketu, of whom the former was one of his teachers [*Bṛi. Up.* vi. 3, 7] and the latter one of his fellow-disciples.

The biography of Yājñavalkya is practically

the cultural history of his country in his times. That part of India was then the home of Vedic culture, and educationally most advanced. Its intellectual life was quickened from various centres, which were being visited by groups of wandering scholars to slake their thirst for learning. Soon after the completion of his education Yājñavalkya appears as one of a small group of such scholars wandering through the country in pursuit of learning, his companions in travel being Śvetaketu Āruṇeya and Soma-Śusma Sātyayajñin. The travelling scholars were met on the way by the learned prince of the times, King Janaka of Videha, who at once raised a discussion on some abstruse topic of ritualism, at which Yājñavalkya fared the best and was rewarded by the king with a gift of 100 cows. But the king, before 'driving away in his car,' was careful to point out the deficiency in the knowledge of them all. This was felt as an insult by the Brāhman scholars with their sense of intellectual superiority. They said: "Surely, this fellow of a Rājanya has out-talked us: come, let us challenge him to a theological discussion!" Yājñavalkya, with the humility that genuine learning gives, said: "We are Brāhmaṇas, and he is a Rājanya: if we were to vanquish him, whom should we say we had vanquished? But if he were to vanquish us, poeple would say of us that a Rājanya had vanquished Brāhmanas: do not think of this!" They approved of his words and desisted from their contemplated challenge, which was against the spirit of genuine culture. But Yājñavalkya, a more sincere seeker after truth, parted company with them and, "mounting his car, drove after the king," whom he soon overtook. King Janaka, moved by his zeal for learning, at once gave him the desired instruction, for which he was promised a boon by his Brāhman pupil. The king, with true nobility and respect for learning, anticipated him with the remarkable exhortation: "Let mine be the privilege of asking questions of thee when I list, Yājñavalkya" [*Satap. Br.* xi. 6, 2].

The distinction that he achieved as a student was followed up by greater distinction won in his later life. He rapidly grew up to be one of the most eminent teachers and thinkers of his times. In the Upanisads, which represent Hindu philosophy at its highest, Yājñavalkya figures as the most distinguished philosopher. His intellectual and spiritual superiority is challenged, but in vain, by the leading philosophers and intellectuals of the times, who were summoned to a Congress specially convened for the purpose by King Janaka of Videha in connexion with his celebration of a horse-sacrifice. The royal invitation was extended to all the learned men of the entire Kuru-Pañchala country, which, as rightly pointed out in the commentary of Śankara, was then "famed for its abundance of learned scholars." A rich reward of 1000 cows with their horns hung with gold coins (five pieces, or pādas, to each) was offered to the one who should be adjudged to be the most learned of the assembly. Yājña-valkya, in self-confidence, without waiting for the judgment, at once appropriated the prize and asked his pupils to carry it off. This assumption of superiority gave the signal for the tournament to begin No less than eight learned champions, one of whom was a lady, entered the lists against Yājñavalkya, who defeated and silenced every one of them in argument. A large part of the *Brihadāraṇyaka Upanisad* is but the record of the transactions of this Philosophical Congress, so to speak, at which were developed and defined, by means of questions and answers, discussion and disputation, the theories and solutions of some of the most intricate problems and mysteries of life.

One of those who challenged Yājñavalkya was his own whilom teacher, Uddālaka Āruni, himself one of the most learned men of the times with a distinguished academic record to his credit. In his youth he wandered far from his native place, the Kuru-Pañchāla country, in quest of truth, and once dwelt for some time in the land of the Madras in the north to seek instruction from their learned scholar Patañchala Kāpya [*Bri. Up.* iii. 7, 1]. At another time we find him "driving out amongst the people of the northern country," and "calling out the timid to a disputation," at which "fear seized the Brāhmaṇs of the nothern people" till they found their champion in their own scholar Svaidāyana Śaunaka [*Śatap. Br.* xi. 4, 1]. He was thus a representative scholar and philosopher of his age, whose academic standing and status are thus indicated by Oldenberg [*Buddha*, p. 396 n]: "When the time shall have come for the inquiries which will have to be made to create order out of the chaotic mass of names of teachers and other celebrities of the Brāhmaṇa period, it may turn out that the most important centre for the formation and diffusion of the Brāhamaṇa doctrine will have to be looked for in Āruni and in the circles which surrounded him." In answer to the question put by his former teacher, Yājñavalkya delivers a profoundly learned discourse, describing the Absolute or the Ātman, the All-pervading, and the Eternal, exterior to which nothing can be. "After that Uddālaka Āruṇi held his peace."

Another disputant was Aśvala, whose learning gained him the high office of Hotṛi priest to King Janaka of Videha. He put to Yājñavalkya both philosophical questions bearing on Mukti, or Deliverance, and practical questions on points of ritualistic worship, and was silenced by his satisfactory answers.

The next disputant was Ārtabhāga, who puts a question on the Senses, their organs and objects, and then the more abstruse questions about death, soul and immortality, which Yājñavalkya preferred to discuss in private and in solitude, and not in an open conference. Hence said he to Ārtabhāga: "Take my hand, my friend. We two *alone* shall best know of this and not in a crowded meeting." Then these two went out and discoursed on the doctrine of Karma. "After that Ārtabhāga held his peace."

Then followed Bhujyu, a fellow-pupil of his whilom teacher Uddālaka Aruṇi, and therefore a man considerably senior to Yājñavalkya, with a question on the destiny of the Pārīkṣitas, as a consequence of the horse-sacrifice performed by them in atonement of their sins. He was satisfied by the answer given.

Further questions are next put by Uṣasta and Kahoḍa on the nature of the Brahman that is immanent and not transcendent, the Ātman that is within all. To the former, who wanted to realise Brahman as one perceived an object, Yājñavalkya's reply is that the Brahman or Ātman is something beyond the sensuous or the objective, something by which the senses themselves are enabled to perceive their objects, and which is therefore incomprehensible to the senses. To the later he delivers the following profoundly moving message: "The Ātman is that which is without and above hunger and thirst, sorrow and passion, decay and death. Realising that Ātman, Brāhmaṇas conquer the desire for progeny, for wealth and possessions and even for heaven, and embrace the life of renunciation as homeless mendicants, subsisting by the strength which the knowledge of Ātman alone gives; then they devote themselves to contemplation till they are ultimately merged in the Brahman!"

The next challenge comes from a woman, Gārgī, the daughter of Vachaknu, who first puts a series of questions culminating in a topic that is beyond the scope of discussion and exposes her own lack of knowledge. She thus keeps silence for a while, but again returns to the fray, saying: "As an heroic youth from Kāśī or Videha bends his unbent bow and takes two deadly arrows in his hand, I have armed myself against thee, O Yājñavalkya, with two questions, which solve for me." She was so sure about the difficulty of the two questions that she openly declared before the learned assembly that, if Yājñavalkya answered them, he would prove himself invincible against all opponents. The two questions were on Brahman, described as Limitless in Time and Space, but in whom exist Time and Space. Yājñavalkya further defines Brahman "as the Akṣara, Indestructible; who is devoid of the attributes pertaining to ordinary matter, such as gross or subtle, great or small; who is not red like fire nor fluid like water; neither shadowy nor dark; not wind, and not ether; not adhesive (unmixed with anything), existing by Itself; without taste, smell, eyes, ears, speech, understanding; without light or breath; without a mouth (door) leading to something else; without size, and neither a measure nor measurable; without inside or outside; and neither consuming nor consumable. This Akṣara Brahman keeps in order and functioning the sun and moon, earth and heaven; moments and hours, days and nights, half-months, months, seasons, and years; He keeps rivers in their courses towards different directions ; and it is He who secures to the doer the fruits of his deeds, and connects causes and effects, though apart in time. That Brahman is unseen, but all-seeing; unheard, but all-hearing; unperceived, but all-perceiving; unknown, but all-knowing; and the primary Principle that enables Vision, Audition, Perception and Cognition". At the conclusion of this discourse Gārgī said: "Venerable Brāhmans, you may consider it a great thing if you can now get off by simply bowing before him. No one, I am sure, can ever even dream of defeating him in any argument concerning Brahaman." And, saying this, she held her peace.

The last of his opponents was Vidagdha Śākalya, who carries on a long discussion, in which he seeks to define Brahman as one that rules in the bodily forms—in love, the sun, sound, etc. Yājña-valkya corrects him by pointing out that what he described was the subordinate puruṣa and not the supreme puruṣa, "who oversteps these puruṣas, separating them from one another and turning them back (*i.e.* inciting them to activity and recalling them)."

His last opponent in argument being thus silenced, Yājñavalkya addressed the assembly thus: "Reverend Brāhmaṇs, whosoever among you desires to do so, may now question me. Or question me, all of you. Or whosoever among you desires it, I shall question him, or I shall question all of you." But those Brāhmans durst not say anything.

The fame of Yājñavalkya as the greatest philosopher of his age was now established. We now find him teaching some of his own teachers. We have already seen how one of these, Uddālaka Āruṇi, himself a distinguished leader of thought, yielded to his whilom pupil in knowledge and argument. Another was the learned prince, Janakà Vaideha [whom we are to consider as occupying the foremost position among the sages of his time (Deussen, *Philosophy of the Upaniṣads*, p. 347)], in discussion with whom Yājñavalkya was able to develop his doctrines. "Like the traveller furnishing himself with a ship or a wagon for a long journey, the king had his mind equipped for the eternal journey of the soul with suitable Upaniṣads or doctrines," imparted to him by his other teachers, named Jitvan, Udaṅka, Barku, Gardabhīvipīta, Satyakāma Jābāla, Vidagdha Śākalya. These had taught him respectively six definitions of Brahman as Speech, Breath, Eye, Ear, Manas and Heart. Yājñavalkya further develops these definitions by pointing out the Upaniṣads or hidden attributes belonging to those six appearances as their "supports" (āyatana), viz. *Prajñā*, belonging to Vāk (for knowledge is conveyed by speech), *Priyam* to Prāṇa, for Life always seeks its own good or satisfaction for its self-reservation, *Satyam* to Eye, which conveys Truth better than the ear, *Anantam* to Ear, Ānanda to Manas, for Thought is the source of Bliss, and Sthiti to Hṛidaya, for in heart rests everything. At the conclusion of each lesson, the King offered the gift of 1000 cows with big bulls like elephants; but Yājñavalkya each time declined the offer on the ground that, under his father's instruction, a teacher could not accept it before he had completed the teaching of his pupil. On another occasion King Janaka, leaving his throne, approached Yājñavalkya, and, bowing to him, requested his instruction. Yājñavalkya hailed the King as one who was self-collected by study of the Upaniṣads, worthy of honour like the gods, wealthy and yet learned by studying the Vedas and listening to Upaniṣadic discourses. Therefore to such a competent person he puts the most difficult question, "Whither will you go after death?" The question could not be answered by the King, and was made the basis of further abstruse instruction by Yājñavalkya upon a theme which baffles human thought to this day [cf. Deussen's candid confession : "Nor have we even to-day any better reply to give" (*Philosophy*, p. 90)]. The substance of his instruction is that "the soul after death goes nowhere where it has not been from the very beginning, nor does it become other than that which it has always been, the one eternal Omnipresent Ātman" (Dussen's *Philosophy*, p. 348). At the conclusion of the instruction the King was so much moved as to lay at the feet of his preceptor the gift of his entire kingdom with himself as his slave!

There is recorded a third occasion on which these two held a philosophical discussion. Here the King first proposes the question, "What serves man for light?" Yajnavalkya explains that, when external light such as sun, moon or fire fails, there shines the inner light of his self or ātman. This Self is defined as "the spirit behind the organs of sense which is essential knowledge and shines within in the heart." That spirit at birth assumes a body and becomes united with all evils, but the evils are left behind at death. A person, as Yājñavalkya further explains, consists of desires. As is his desire, so is his will: as is his will, so is his deed; and whatever deed he does, that he will reap. To whatever object a man's own mind is attached, to that he goes strenuously together with his deed; and, having obtained the complete consequences of whatever deed he does on earth, he returns again from that world (which is the temporary reward of his deed) to this world of action. But as to the man who does not desire, who, not desiring, freed from desires, is satisfied in his desires, or desires the Self only, his vital spirits do not depart elsewhere,—being Brahman, he goes to Brahman. When all desires which once entered his heart are undone, then does the mortal become immortal, then he obtains Brahman, with his body cast off like the skin of a snake. If a man understands the Self thus, saying "I am He," what could he wish or desire that he should pine after the body? Knowing this, the people of old did not wish for offspring. What shall we do with offspring, they said, we who have this Self and this world of Brahman? At the end of these words "than which deeper. finer. more noble, were never uttered by human lips" (as remarked by Deussen), the King repeated his previous gift, saying: "Sir, I give you the Videhas, and also myself, to be together your slaves" [*Bṛi. Up.* iv. 1-4].

Nor was Yājñavalkya in the least unprepared to apply his teachings to himself. He lived the philosophy he preached. His theory as to the means of self-realisation, the quest of the Brahman, the Ultimate Truth, led him to the crowning act of his life, the renunciation of the world and adoption of the mendicant's life of homelessness. This brings us to a most interesting episode in his life as related in the *Bri. Upaniṣad* [iv. 5], which states how Yājñavalkya had two wives, Maitreyī and Kātyāyanī by name, of whom the former was conversant with Brahman and the latter had only the knowledge ordinary women have. Resolving to leave the life of a householder for that of the forest, he one day called his wife Maitreyī and announced his intention thus: "Maitreyī, verily I am going away from this my house (into the forest). Forsooth, let me make a settlement between thee and that Kātyāyanī." Maitreyī said: "My Lord, if this whole earth, full of wealth, belonged to me, tell me, should I be immortal by it, or no?" "No," replied Yājñavalkya, "like the life of rich people will be thy life. But there is no hope of immortality by wealth." And Maitreyī said: "What should I do with that by which I do not become immortal? What my Lord knoweth of immortality, tell that clearly to me." Yājñavalkya replied: "Thou who art truly dear to me, thou hast increased what is dear to me in thee. Therefore, if thou like, lady, I will explain it to thee, and mark well what I say." Then Yājñavalkya proceeds to explain to her his doctrine of Ātman thus: "The husband is dear to the wife not for the husband's sake, but for the sake of the Ātman: similarly is the wife dear to the husband not for her sake, but for the sake of the Ātman. So also sons, wealth, Brahmaṇs, Kṣatriyas, gods, Vedas and the universe, are all dear, not on their own account, but for the sake of the Self." The meaning is that all objects and relations of the universe exist for us, and are known and loved by us only in so far as they enter into our consciousness, which comprehends in itself all the objects of the universe and has nothing outside of itself. Therefore it is stated further: "The Self in truth we should comprehend, should reflect upon, O Maitreyī. He who has seen, heard, comprehended and known the Self, by him this entire universe is known." "As the notes of a drum, a conch-shell, or a lute have no existence in themselves, and can only be received when the instrument that produces them is struck, so all objects and relations of the universe are known by him who knows the Ātman. From this great Being were breathed forth, like clouds of smoke from fire kindled with damp fuel, the Vedas and other subjects of knowledge, nay, food and drink, even this world, and the other world, and all creatures. As all waters have their meeting place in the sea, all touch in the skin, all tastes in the tongue, all odours in the nose, all colours in the eye, all sounds in the ear, all precepts in the mind, all knowledge in the heart, all actions in the hands, all movements in the feet, and all the Vedas in speech. As a mass of salt has neither inside nor outside, but is altogether a mass of taste, thus, indeed, has that Self neither inside nor outside, but is altogether a mass of knowledge." After this Yājñavalkya propounds the paradoxical proposition—"after death there is no consciousness"; whereupon poor Maitreyī interrupts him, saying: "Here, Sir, thou hast landed me in utter bewilderment. Indeed, I do not understand him (the Self)." Yājñavalkya assured her: "O Maitreyi, I say nothing that is bewildering," and then proceeded to explain his meaning further with the words: "For where there is, as it were, a duality (in reality there is not), there one sees the other, smells, hears, addresses, comprehends, and knows the other; but where everything has become to him his own self, how should he smell, see, hear, address, understand, or know any one at all? How should he know him, through whom he knows all this, how should he know the knower?" Then saying, "Thus, O Maitreyī, thou hast been instructed," Yājñavalkya went away into the forest! [*Br. Up.* iv. 6]. Philosophy in India meant something to be realised and lived, and not merely to be studied. "The knowledge of Brahman is not an understanding of pantheistic doctrines such as may be obtained by reading *The Sacred Books of the East* in an easy chair, but a realisation in all senses of personal identity with the universal spirit, in the light of which all material attachments and fetters fall away" [Sir Charles Eliot, *Hinduism and Buddhism*, vol. i. p. 75].

Thus did Yājñavalkya withdraw himself from life and its interests to plunge into the Unknown, but his teachings lived after him in the memory of generations of teachers and students succeeding one another, by a system of oral tradition to which we owe the conservation of our entire sacred literature. His teachings in some important particulars supply the basis upon which Hindu Philosophy has evolved and expanded through the ages. They may be summed up in the three following propositions:

(1) *The Ātman is the knowing subject within us.* As we have already seen, Yājñavalkya describes it once as "the spirit consisting of knowledge, *vijñānamaya*, shining within in the heart, the light that enlightens when sun, moon, stars, fire, and even the guidance of sound, fail, the light of lights" (*Br. Up.* iv. 3, 2-7).

(2) *The Ātman, as the knowing subject, can never become an object for us, and is therefore itself unknowable.* It is to be noted that there are statements made by Yājñavalkya which apparently regard Ātman as an object of knowledge: *e.g.* "the Ātman should be seen, heard, comprehended and reflected upon" [*Bṛ. Up.* ii. 4, 5]; or the representation of Brahman as "Being, Thought

and Bliss" (*sat-chid-ānanda*) [*Bṛ. Up.* ii. 1, 19]. But these apparently positive descriptions are really negative attributes from the standpoint of experience : the 'being' of Ātman is no being as revealed in experience, while the 'bliss' can be understood only as the negation of all suffering, for *ato 'nyad ārtam*, "what is dinstinct from Him is full of suffering" [*Bṛ. Up.* iii. 4, 2]. The knowledge of Brahman is thus radically different from ordinary knowledge, the knowledge of empirical reality, distinguished as *avidyā* (*amṛitaṃ satyena chhannam*—the immortal or ātman is veiled by empirical reality). Ordinary knowledge implies the duality of subject and object, and hence Brahman, as the All-comprehending Unity, is unknowable. Hence he can only be defined negatively by the expression '*neti, neti*,' etc. Empirical predicates cannot be ascribed to him : the entire empirical order of things is subject to the laws of Space, Time and Causality, but Brahman is Spaceless, Timeless and Independent of Causality [*Bṛ. Up.* iii, 8, 7].

(3) *The Ātman is the Sole Reality* (*satyam, satyasya satyam*). "There is no second outside of him, no other distinct from him" [*Bṛ. Up.* iv. 3, 23-30]. As Deussen explains it, "There is not, and never can be, for us reality outside of the ātman (a universe outside of our consciousness)." Here we have enunciated, to the immortal honour of the Upaniṣads and Yājñavalkya, the fundamental position in all Philosophy or Religion—the thought that the Universe (comprising both

the external universe and the sum total of our own inner perceptions) is only Appearance or Illusion, and not Reality. This Illusion must be pierced through by the sharp sword of knowledge, in which consists Deliverance. We all need release from this existence, which is the realm of ignorance. Thus the knowledge of Ātman is itself, not merely helps us to attain, Emancipation.

This doctrine of Ātman as the sole reality is no doubt first uttered in the famous Ṛigvedic proposition [*Ṛv*. i. 164, 46]—"*Ekam Sad Viprā bahudhā vadanti*: Him the Sole Reality the Sages describe under various names." "All plurality, consequently all proximity in space, all succession in time, all relation of cause and effect, all interdependence of subject and object, rests only upon words, is a mere matter of words, *vāchārambhaṇa*" [*Chh. Up*. vi. 1, 4]. But Yājñavalkya was the first to grasp this conception of the Ātman in its complete subjective and scientific precision, and thus ranks as one of the founders of Upaniṣadic Philosophy. We also owe to him another great contribution to human thought, viz., the recognition of the identity of what we usually call God and Soul-the cosmical principle of the universe and the psychical—the recognition of one Ātman, our innermost individual being, as the Brahman, the inmost being of universal nature and of all her phenomena, as expressed in the well-known formulae, "*Aham Brahma asmi*, I am Brahman" [*Br. Up*. i. 4, 10], "*Tat tvam asi*, That art Thou" [*Chh. Up*. vi. 8, 7],

"*Sa vā ayam ātmā brahma*, "Truly the Brahman is this Ātman" [*Bṛ. Up*. iv. 4, 5], and in other passages already cited. In this connexion, we may also note another necessary consequence of this teaching of Yājñavalkya, the assignment of sacrificial rites, insisted on by the older religion, to their proper place in the scheme of life. The value of the sacrificial cult is thus given by Yājñavalkya, to quote one among several passages: "Of a truth, Of Gārgī, he who does not know this Imperishable One, and in this world sacrifices and distributes alms and does penance for many thousands of years, wins thereby only finite good" [*Bṛ. Up*. iii, 8, 10].

There are a few other minor biographical details about the sage which may now be referred to. The concluding passage of the *Bṛihadāranyaka Upaniṣad* [vi. 5, 4] attributes to Yājñavalkya the White Yajus. There may be a question as to whether this supposed authorship of Yājñavalkya implies that he actually composed or only that he collected and compiled the sacred code of the Vājasaneyins. The question seems to be settled by the fact that at the time of Pāṇini (which, according to the well-known Indian authority, Sir R. G. Bhandarkar, may be roughly fixed at seventh century B.C.) that code was regarded as the work of Yājñavalkya himself and not as a work handed down by tradition among a school of teachers and disciples, as was very often the case with reference to most of our older Sanskrit works. A sūtra of Panini, as interpreted by the *Vārttika* [iv. 3, 105], shows that the *Śatapatha Brāhmana* was regarded in Pāṇini's time as a work which was, firstly, more modern in date than other Brāhmaṇas, and, secondly, produced by an individual author and not simply proclaimed (*prokta*) by him, or constituting the traditional property of an ancient Vedic śākhā bearing his name. The evidence of Pāṇini and Kātyāyana as to Yājñavalkya being a somewhat later or more modern ṛiṣi is confirmed by a curious passage in the *Gṛihya Śūtra* of Āpastamba (about 500 B.C.), in which Śevetaketu, the contemporary and co-disciple of Yājñavalkya, is referred to as a rare example amongst the *men of later ages* (when brahmacharya rules were not strictly observed), of a scholar who became a ṛiṣi by his knowledge of the *Veda* [i. 2, 5, 6]. We have a few other biographical touches preserved: In the *Śatapatha Brāhmaṇa*, Yājñavalkya is sometimes represented as a somewhat recalcitrant priest, to whom are attributed some new views and doctrines. He protested against the priests' new demand that the benefits of the sacrifices should accrue in part to the priest, and said: "How can people have faith in this? Whatever be the blessing for which the priests pray, this blessing is for the worshipper (sacrificer) alone" [i. 3, 1, 26]. The essential nobility of his soul is expressed in his prayer to the Sun: "*Carcho me dehi*, Give me Light," which strikes a completely spiritual note as compared with the materialistic flavour of prayers like—"Give me cows!" [i. 9, 3, 16].

In conclusion, we may note the educational and cultural conditions and opportunities of the country, as illustrated in the life of Yājñavalkya. First, there were the small domestic schools, or homes of learning, run by a teacher who admitted to his family as many boarder-pupils as he could manage. When their education is finished after several years of disciplined life, they generally return home and settle down as householders. But the more earnest students, in whom love of knowledge was like a passion, would wander about through the country, seeking out for their satisfaction other more distinguished teachers in different seats of learning. Circles of such wandering scholars were some of the common sights of the times. In the course of their wanderings in quest of learning they would naturally meet other scholars and engage in exchange of views and, often, in animated discussions. Some times such discussions were not due to accidental meetings, but were deliberately challenged in a foreign region by the visiting scholars, who would even throw down a prize for victory. Thus education, beside that imparted by the settled schools, was very largely spread and promoted in its higher stages by learned debates among scholars of different provinces, who would seek such opportunities of establishing their philosophical positions or scientific theories, and thereby their intellectual status and eminence, in the realm of letters. It was also a very happy sign of the times that Learning did not fail to receive her due tribute from Wealth. The Aristocracies of Brain and Bullion lived in happy harmony and mutual esteem. Brāhmans, proud of their intellectual lineage and their own acquired knowledge, were not slow to receive instruction wherever found. They cheerfully accepted pupilage under Kṣatriyas who could teach. In the age of Yājñavalkya a large part in the intellectual life of the country was played by kings, who threw themselves into it with an enthusiasm that testifies to their genuine democratic feeling, their sense of universal brotherhood in the kingdom of spirit, of which all were entitled to be free citizens. Some of the kings were themselves leaders of thought and drew students for instruction in the special truths of which they were the repositories: such were Janaka of Videha, Ajātaśatru of Kāsī, Pravahaṇa Jaivali of the Pañchāla country, or Aśvapati Kaikeya. But, besides directly promoting learning as teachers, they also indirectly contributed to it by their generous patronage of learning, in which King Janaka was foremost. His only enjoyment was not the pleasures of the usual royal hunt or chase, but the company of the learned, as the Emperor Asoka in later times replaced the royal pleasure-tours by tours for religious objects and pilgrimages. On festive occasions King Janaka would summon Congresses of learned men from different parts and lavishly reward skill in debate and proved intellectual superiority, while his own gain was the feast of reason they provided. Thus gatherings of learned men at the courts of kings constituted another of the agencies by which intellectual life was fostered in the country. Lastly, it is worthy of note that women were not denied their share in that intellectual life. They were admitted to public debates in learned conferences, in which they could play active parts: they developed philosophical positions of their own, which they were free to expound and establish in such conferences; whilst at home, in the privacy and seclusion of domestic life, they could enjoy a complete fellowship with their husbands in culture and learning, and join in a common investigation of the ultimate problems and truths in a common spiritual life. This liberty of life and learning enjoyed by the women of ancient India ought to be recalled in later times. It was in this atmosphere of freedom and spirituality that the human mind in India was enabled to achieve some of the greatest triumphs in the pursuit of Truth and the solution of the mysteries of existence.

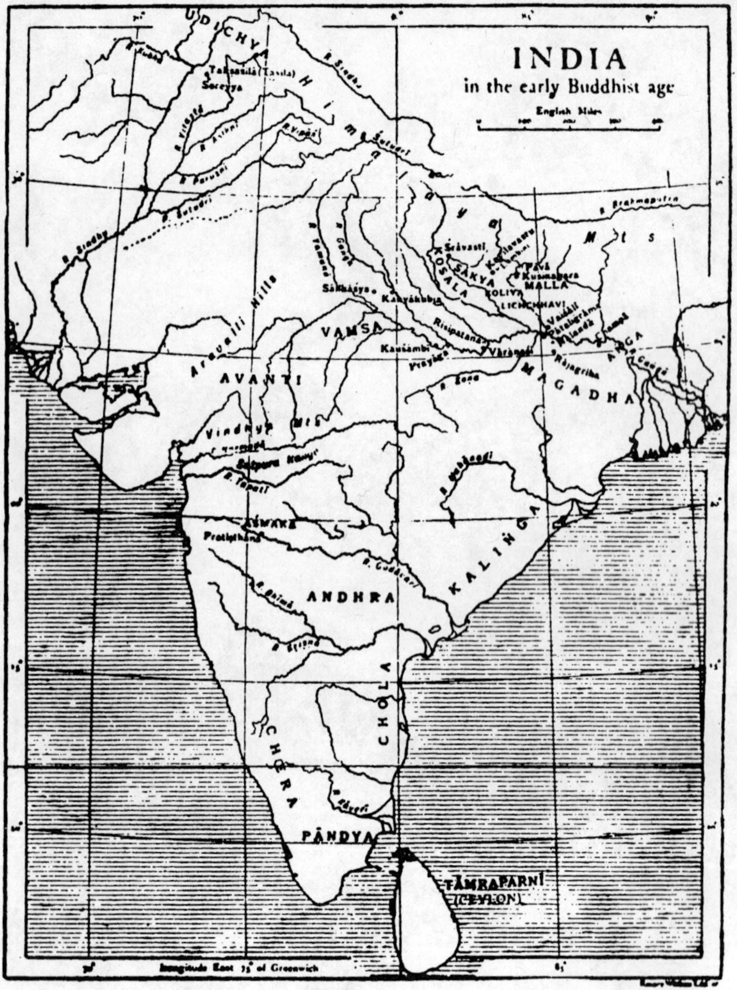

INDIA
in the early Buddhist age
English Miles
UDICHYA
Himalaya Mts
Takkasilā (Taxila)
Soreyya
R. Sindhu
R. Sutudri
R. Paruṣṇī
R. Sutudri
R. Yamunā
R. Gaṅgā
R. Brahmaputra
Śrāvastī
KOSALA
SAKYA
KOLIYA
MALLA
LICHCHHAVI
Pāvā
Kusinagara
Saṅkāsya
Kanyākubja
Risipatana
Vārāṇasī
Vaiśālī
Rājagriha
Champā
VAMSA
Kauśāmbī
Prayāga
R. Sona
MAGADHA
ANGA
Aravalli Hills
AVANTI
Vindhya Mts
Satpura Range
R. Tāpatī
AŚMAKA
Pratiṣṭhāna
R. Godāvarī
ANDHRA
R. Bhīmā
R. Kṛṣṇā
KALIṄGA
CHOLA
CHERA
R. Kāverī
PĀNDYA
TĀMRAPARNĪ
(CEYLON)
Longitude East 75° of Greenwich

THE BUDDHA

ANCIENT India, with its extraordinarily vast and varied literature, lacks in a marked degree historical records properly so called. This is probably because Hindu thought did not attach the value which is given in the West to life and its transitory interests. The great men of Indian history counted only for the ideals they stood for, and not in the personal aspects and details of their lives. Records are kept of what they thought, said, or taught, but not directly of what they did. The truth weighed more than the truth-seeker, the teaching more than the teacher. This is how the vast literature of Brāhmaṇas and Upaniṣads, while replete with descriptions of the beliefs and practices of their sages, the doctrines they taught and the ceremonies and sacrifices they performed, are completely silent about the details of their individual, personal lives. Similarly, even in later times, the works of Vālmikī, Vyāsa or Kālidāsa, the doctrines of Śankara or Rāmānuja, Kabīr or Nānak, are widely studied and followed, giving rise in some cases to extensive commentaries; but how few are the details known in their individual careers! Biography as a subject is practically unknown in old Indian literature. But, as regards this deficiency in historical sense, it may be said that it is to some extent characteristic of Science, of which the students care more for what is true and established in theory and useful in practice than for the exploded hypotheses and defective instruments of the past. In fact, it is easy to exaggerate the value of historical treatment of thought and art. Dr. Bosanquet [*Gifford Lectures*, 1912, p. 78] gives a good, well-merited warning against the prevailing tendencies: "History is a hybrid form of experience incapable of any considerable degree of being, or trueness. The doubtful story of successive events cannot amalgamate with the complete interpretation of the social mind, of art, or of religion. The great things which are necessary in themselves become within the narrative contingent, or ascribed by most doubtful assumptions of insight, to this actor or that on the historical stage. The study of Christianity is the study of a great world-experience: the assignment to individuals of a share in its development is a problem for scholars whose conclusions, though of considerable human interest, can never be of supreme importance." With reference to the great document of the Bhagavadgītā, few among the millions of its readers care for questions about its date, authorship, authenticity and textual accuracy. It is like the Tāj, in the appreciation of whose beauty are forgotten the architects who designed or the kings who paid for it.

Thus, even with regard to a towering personality like Gautama Buddha, whose teachings are followed by nearly a fourth of the human race, we have hardly any biography properly so called, except such as can be constructed by piecing together scattered bits of information given in connexion with his teachings. Some works much later than his time, like the *Lalita-Vistara* in Sanskrit, aim at presenting the life of the Master not on the lines of what he actually was and did, but on those of what a Buddha is expected to be and do: they may be compared to the *Paradise Regained* in the abundance of the miraculous and supernatural introduced. More trustworthy details of his life can be gleaned from some of the older Pāli works, notably the *Vinaya* and the *Suttas*, in connexion with the circumstances they relate in which the Buddha laid down a particular rule or preached a particular sermon. Both these sources of the Buddha's life have however to be carefully studied and compared, specially to find out the facts which are common to them and therefore much more reliable, not exactly as the actual facts of the Buddha's life, but as those at least taken to be such in the belief of the earlier Buddhists. As Dr. Rhys Davids well points out [*Buddhism*, p. 16], we should not "reject entirely the evidence of any witness who believes in the miraculous," while it is "absured to imagine that the life of Gautama is all a fiction, and that the Buddhist philosophy, or the still powerful order of Buddhist mendicant friars, could have arisen from the misunderstood development of some solar myth"—a theory of some unbelievers which has been very effectively disposed of by Oldenberg [*Buddha*, English trans. 1882, pp. 72 foll.]. Dr. Rhys Davids further affirms : "There was certainly a historical basis for the Buddhist legend ; and, if it be asked whether it is at all possible to separate the true from the false, I would reply that the difficulty, though great, is apt to be exaggerated. The retailers of these legends are not cunning forgers, but simple-minded men, with whose modes of thought we can put ourselves more or less *en rapport*." After stripping the story of the miraculous and mythical elements, what remains as the historical nucleus[1] will enable us to present the life of the Buddha as an actual human being, with concrete and realistic details, as compared with the obscure and shadowy personalities we read of in Vedic literature.

[1] On this general question of the treatment of Buddhist tradition, compare the following remarks of Geiger [*Mahāvaṃsa*, Introd., p. xiv] : "I do not conceal from myself that this judgement of the situation lays itself open to the reproach that our method is simply to elminate from the tradition all the miraculous stories and consider what is left over as authentic history. But I think Windisch has shown admirably how, in fact, in the Buddhist tradition, around a relatively small nucleus all kinds of additions have collected in time, by which events, originally simple, are withdrawn gradually into the region of the marvellous. 'But we must not therefore pour away the child with the bath. Here, too, the task of Science is to lay bare the grain of truth ; not only this, but she must seek the meaning and significance of the mythical crown of rays that has gathered round the nucleus. For the mythical is often the covering of deep thoughts.' "

The Buddha was born the son of Śuddhodana, the Rājā (chief or king) of the Ksatriya clan of the Śākyas, in about 623 B.c. according to the latest theory.[1] It is not known definitely whether the Śākya state was a kingship or a sort of a republic. On the one hand we read of a neighbouring king. Pasenadi of Kosala, suing for a girl of pure Śākyan blood for his wife, and of the Śākyas, proud of their birth, meeting that request halfway by sending the daughter of a Śākya by a slave-woman: we read also on the other hand, of the Assembly of the Śākyas transacting the judicial and administrative business of the clan

[1] The theory is the result of the latest widely accepted reaching of certain lines in the famous Hāthigumpha Cave Inscription of Khāravela, according to which King Khāravela comes about 178 years after Chandragupta Maurya (322 B.C., or 325 B.C. according to some). We are further told that he came 305 years after a Nanda king, who would thus have reigned in about 452 B.C. Accepting the Puranic figures for the duration of the reigns of the kings of the period, we find that it was Mahānandin who ruled in 452 B.C. Thence we come to the important fact that his predecessors in the same Śaiśunāga dynasty, the Kings Bimbisāra and Ajātaśatru, who were both contemporaries of the Buddha, reigned between 611-556 B.C. Thus we are in a position to accept the traditional Ceylon date for the death of the Buddha, viz. 544 or 543 B.C.; and, since he lived for about 80 years, the date of his birth works out at about 623 B.C. [See *JBORS*, December 1917, for the edition of the inscription by the learned scholars, Messrs. Jayaswal and Banerji; V. A. Smith's article in the *JRAS*, July 1918, and *Oxford History of India*, pp. 48 and 58 n.] Tradition makes Ajātaśatru usurp the throne when the Buddha was 72 years old (see Kern), and in that case he would reign from 551 B.C.

in their common mote-hall at Kapilavastu[1] [*Ang. N.* iii. 57]. Be that as it may, there is no doubt that the Buddha was born of a wealthy and aristocratic family, his father being sometimes spoken of as the Rāja as well as his cousin Bhaddiya.[2] Tradition treats the Buddha as a born prince, but it may be interested in magnifying his wealth and social position to magnify the value of his renunciation.

The Śākya territory was bounded towards the east by the Lichchhavi Confederation and Magadha kingdom, towards the west by the Kosala kingdom, and on the northern side by the river Rohiṇī, upon which it was dependent for irrigation.

[1] In the *Ambaṭṭha Sutta* of the Dīgha Nikāya there is a reference to the Śākyas, young and old, occupying grand seats for deliberation in the hall. In the *Sonadaṇḍa* and *Kūṭadanta Suttas* are some passages where Brāhmaṇs, discussing the Buddha's claims to respect, state that he is born of a noble and wealthy, but not a royal, family. In the *Aggañña Suttanta* occurs the following passage : "Now the Sākiyas are become the vassals of King Pasenadi. They render to him homage and respectful salutation, they rise and do him obeisance, and treat him with ceremony." Does not this clearly indicate that the Śākya state came to be absorbed in the neighbouring powerful monarchy of Kosala ? This view is further supported by *Sam. N.* i. 79, where King Pasenadi is mentioned as the chief, mahārāja, among five other rājās like the Śākya nobles.

[2] In Chullavagga (vii. 1) he is represented, in renouncing the world, as saying : "Wait whilst I hand over the *rajja* to my sons and my brothers." The doubt is as to the exact meaning of the words *Rāja* and *Rajja*, which may refer to the position, temporary and elective, of a Roman consul, rather than to the hereditary position of a king. Śuddhodana or Bhaddiya was a Rājā, but not a Mahārāja like Ajātaśatru.

This was a fertile cause of feud with the Koliya clan on the other side of the river. The feud was composed for a time by a matrimonial alliance, by which the Śākya chief, Śuddhodana, married the two daughters of the Koliya chief, Mahā-māyā and Mahā-Prajāpatī Gautamī by name, of whom the former gave birth to the Buddha at the age of forty-five, under the shade of a sāl tree in the pleasant grove of Lumbinī on her way to her parents' place at Devadaha. The site of the birth-place has been traced by an Asokan pillar bearing the inscription—"Here the Great One was born."

The mother and the child were sent back to Śuddhodana's place at Kapilavastu. Five days after his birth the child Bodhisattva was given the name Siddhārtha ; seven days afterwards he lost his mother, and he was brought up by her sister, Prajāpatī.

He was sent to a primary school to learn the three R's under a master named Viśvāmitra, whom, according to tradition, he confounds by his knowledge, already possessed, of various styles of writing. He is next taught by eight other Brāhman teachers, viz. "Rāma and Dhaja, Lakkhaṇa and Manti, Yañña and Suyāma, Subhoga and Sudatta," and also "the Brāhman Sabbamitta of high lineage in the land of Udichcha (north-west), a philologist and grammarian, well-read in the six Vedāṅgas, whom Śuddhodana sent for, and handed over the boy to his charge, to be taught" [*Mil. Pañh.* iv. 6, 3].

Nor was he inattentive to physical culture. The legends represent him as skilled in "the twelve arts" and especially in archery, like Arjuna of old, and he proved his superiority to all Śākya youths in open challenge. As in the story of Arjuna, the price of his victory was the hand of the Koliya princess, Yaśodharā, daughter of his cousin, Suprabuddha, to whom he was married at sixteen. One of the beaten youths was another cousin of his, Devadatta, who could never forget this discomfiture, and grew up to be the chief enemy of the Buddha in the world.

He continued his married life for more than ten years, till a son was born to him, known as Rāhula. That was the occasion for great rejoicing in the city, but to him for much pensive thought, as it brought home to him the tie that bound him to the world. He received the news of his son's birth at a garden on the river-side, and in the ovation given him while returning home he was specially struck by the song of a maiden, his cousin, Kisā Gotami —"Happy the father, happy the mother, happy the wife of such a son and husband." The word 'happy,' however, bore a different message to him. It reminded him of the real happiness which lay in 'freedom,' in deliverance from the bondage of desire, sin, sorrow and transmigration. Thus the girl taught him the highest truth and received as her reward from him his necklace of pearls, which the poor girl foolishly took to be a lovetoken from him!

That very night, in his twenty-ninth year, it is

said that Gautama "wandered from home into homelessness." But there are different versions given of the story of his renunciation and the circumstances that led up to it. The majority represent him as being carefully segregated in an atmosphere of happiness from all that may mar it—the sight of such ills of life as disease, decay and death. But the plan miscarried under divine providence. By chance he encountered successively the shape of each of those ills, and also of what struck him as the remedy—the figure of a monk before him. But the more correct version is perhaps that which claims to give the Buddha's own account of the incident. In one passage, after describing the wealth and comfort in which he lived with three different palaces in the three seasons, hot, cold and rainy, at his disposal, the Buddha was wondering how people shrink from the sight of old age, sickness or death. He thought: "I also am subject to decay and am not free from the power of old age, sickness and death. Is it right that I should feel horror, repulsion and disgust when I see another in such plight? And when I reflected thus, my disciples, all the joy of life which there is in life died within me." In the same strain the Buddha delivers himself in another passage: "Then I said to myself: 'How now is this, that I, subject to birth, to growth and decay, to disease, to death, to sorrow and to stain, should only seek after that which also is subject to birth, growth and decay, disease, death, sorrow and stain?' And so, disciples, after a time, while still young, a black-haired lad in my youthful prime, just come to budding manhood's years, against the wishes of father and mother weeping and lamenting, I shore off hair and beard, and, garbing myself in robes of yellow, went forth from home, vowed henceforth to the homeless life" [*Majjhima Nikāya*, vol. ii. p. 5, tr. Sīlāchāra]. In another place occurs the following statement: "Cramped and confined is household life, a den of dust; but the life of the homeless one is as the open air of heaven! Hard is it for him who bides at home to live out as it should be lived the Holy Life in all its perfection, in all its purity! How, if I cut off hair and beard and, in garb of yellow, leave home behind and vow myself to the homeless life?" [*ib.* p. 99]. These passages indicate that it was not the mere accidental sight of cases of sickness, infirmity or death that wrought the revolution in the mind of the Bodhisattva and made him loathe and renounce wordly life. What probably happened was that this kind of circumstance only aggravated the already operative tendencies of his mind towards such a renunciation. But apart from the tendencies of a mind deeply sensible to the mysteries of sorrow and death, there were the characteristic tendencies in Indian thought and life at their highest level, which made renunciation of the world in quest of truth a common phenomenon even among the well-to-do classes of society. The Buddha only trod what was the beaten track for the seekers after truth in ancient

India. The situation has been well grasped by that renowned Western student of Buddhism, Dr. Rhys Davids: "He was probably not the first—he was certainly not the last—who in the midst of prosperity and comfort, has felt a yearning and a want which nothing could satisfy, and which have robbed of their charm all earthly gains and hopes. This vague dissatisfaction deepens with every fresh proof of the apparent vanity of life, and does not lose but gains in power when, as is reported in the case of Gautama, it arises more from sympathy with the sorrows of others than from any personal sorrow of one's own. At last the details of daily life become insupportable; and the calm life of the hermit troubled with none of these things seems a haven of peace, where a life of self-denial and earnest meditation may lead to some solution of the strange enigmas of life" [*Buddhism*, p. 30].

The important point to be remembered in this connexion, which is apt to be overlooked, is that the Buddha renounced the world not in old age, but in youth, not out of the surfeit of wordly enjoyments, but in full capacity and relish for them—not in penury, with nothing to lose, but in plenty, with means of satisfying every want. This point is developed in the explanation the Buddha himself gives of his renunciation: "I also, ye monks, before I had attained to Enlightenment, as yet not fully enlightened, still striving after Enlightenment,—myself subject to birth, growth and decay, sickness and death, pain and impurity, sought after what also is subject to these, viz. wife and children, slaves male and female, goats and sheep, fowls and swine, elephants, cattle, horses, mares, gold and silver! Then, ye monks, the thought came to me: 'What, then, am I doing? Myself subject to birth, growth and decay, sickness death, pain, impurity, and seeking also what is subject to these—how if I seek the birthless, ageless, diseaseless, deathless and the stainless incomparable surety, the extinction of illusion!' And, ye monks, after some time, while still in my first bloom, shining, dark-haired, in the enjoyment of happy youth, in the first years of manhood, against the wish of weeping and wailing parents, with shorn hair and beard, clothed in ragged raiment, I went forth from home to homelessness." The same confession is also made by the Buddha to Mahānāma, his cousin, on his accession to the leadership of the Śākya state: "And I, Mahānāma, before my full Awakening, clearly perceived the wretchedness of desires, but, not finding happiness or aught better outside of desires and evil things, I knew not to turn away from following after them" [*Maj. N.* i. 91 *sqq.*].

The nobility and utter frankness of these words, in which the Buddha disclaims any superhuman character for himself, but owns fully to the frailties of his kind, are themselves superhuman. As Paul Dahlke well remarks [*Buddhist Eassys*, p. 15]: "Never before did founder of religion speak like this. One who thus speaks needs not allure with hopes of heavenly joy. One who speaks like this of himself attracts by that power with which the truth attracts all who enter her domain."

Neither was the Buddha singular nor superhuman in the mere fact of his renunciation of the world. Examples of such renunciation were very usual and numerous in India of his times. The typical Hindu thought is uttered by Yājñavalkya: "The intelligent and wise desire not posterity: what are descendants to us, whose home is the Ātman? They relinquish the desire for children, the struggle for wealth, the pursuit of worldly weal, and go forth as mendicants" [*Bṛ. Up.*]. Thus asceticism was a necessary consequence of the Vedic doctrine. In the period of the Brāhmaṇas and Upaniṣads we come acrosss ascetics as wandering scholars eager for discussion and lessons from renowned teachers who have their own systems of both thought and discipline. Thus these bands of ascetics are afterwards organised into regular communities or confraternities, sects or orders following their respective teachers and leaders. In the Buddha's time the country was full of such religious brotherhoods. In the Brahmajāla Sutta [*Dīg. Nik.* i.] as many as sixty-two different systems of 'erroneous doctrine' are criticised by the Buddha himself, while in some Jain works their number is stated to be 363. They were broadly distinguished under two classes, the Brāhmaṇas and Samaṇas. The former comprised sects known as the Titthiyas, Ājīvikas, Nigaṇṭhas, Muṇḍaśāvakas, Jaṭilakas, Paribbājakas, Māgaṇḍikas, Tedaṇḍikas, Eka-sāṭakas [one-robers (*Sam. N.* i. 777)], Aviruddhakas, Gotamakas (a sect founded by another Gotama), Devadhammikas, Charakas, Achelakas, etc. [see *JRAS*, 1898, p. 197, and Sutta-Nipāta], and counted the six famous teachers, contemporaries[1] of the Buddha, called Pūraṇa Kassapa, Makkhali Gosāla (founder of the Ājīviksa), Ajita, Pakudha-Kachchāyana, Sañjaya and Nigaṇṭha-Nātaputta, as also others known as Bāvarī of Assaka territory in the Deccan, Sela, Chaṇkin, Tārukkha, Pokkharasāti, Jānussoṇi, Todeyya and the like. These Brāhman teachers were agnostics or materialists, and described as Vādaśīlas (disputatious), Lokāyatas, Vaitaṇḍikas (casuists and sophists), Tevijjas (versed in the three Vedas or Vidyās), and so forth. As regards the second order of ascetics, the Samaṇas, there are mentioned four kinds, the Magga-jinas, Magga-desins, Magga-jīvins and Magga-dūsins, disputes among whom split them into many more schools, numbering sixty-three, which were designated as Diṭṭhis or *heresies* in the Buddha's time.

It was into this world of ascetics that the young Gautama resolves upon his entrance.

On the full moon night of Āṣāḷha the prince

[1] These are known as the six *Titthakaras* (theorisers), who were much older than the Buddha. Cf. *Sam. N.* i. 69 : "For (as compared with them) master Gotama is young in years and is a novice in the life of religion". This is said by King Pasenadi of Kosala, whom again we find venerating the Buddha as one eighty years old like himself in *Maj. N.* ii. 124. Thus the king was one of the oldest friends and followers of the Buddha.

rose from his bed, had a last look at his sleeping wife and son, and left the palace on what was perhaps the most noteworthy journey ever made by mortal, every step of which has since been marked by costly and artistic monuments, which successive generations of pilgrims have smothered in flowers! His charioteer Chhanna saddled for him his favourite courser Kaṇṭhaka, whereon he rode away from the city till he came to the river Anomā beyond the Koliyan country, which he leaped over with his steed. Then alighting, he sent back both the groom and the horse, shore off hair and beard with his sword and exchanged his fine Benares silks for the yellow robes of the monk. Then, taking a week's rest in the mango grove of Anupiya, he travelled in one day to Rājagṛiha, the capital of Magadha and its King Seṇiya Bimbisāra, in the hope that in the valley of the Ganges he would find better teachers than among the rough wits of the Śākya country. A legend relates that King Bimbisāra, one day looking out from his palace, saw the Buddha, and was so struck by his appearance that he visited him and offered him his whole kingdom, which was of course refused.

The mendicant's life was by no means an easy one for a born prince. When he tried to eat his first meal collected by begging in the city, "his stomach turned, and he felt as if his inwards were on the point of coming out by his mouth," "for in that existence he had never before so much as seen such fare," till by self-admonition he overcame his feeling of "distress at that repulsive food."

Rājagṛiha in the caves of its hills afforded convenient accommodation, neither too near nor too far from the town or sources of alms, to hermits, to one of whom, Āḷāra Kālāma, the Buddha first attached himself as his disciple. He was evidently a renowned sage of the times. A story is told of his great powers of concentration: he would sit in contemplation on the road-side and remain perfectly unconscious of a caravan of 500 carts rattling past him [*Mahā. Par. Sutta*, iv. 35]. He taught to Gautama the doctrine of Nothingness. Gautama describes his progress thus: "Very speedily I learned the doctrine, and so far as concerns uttering with mouth and lips the words, 'I know, I understand,' I and others with me knew the word of wisdom and the ancient lore. Then the thought occurred to me, 'when Āḷāra Kālāma declares: "Having myself realised and known this doctrine, I abide in the attainment thereof," it cannot all be a mere profession of faith; surely Āḷāra Kālāma sees and knows this doctrine."

Knowledge in ancient India was not a mere matter for memory, study or intellectual apprehension: it was something to be realised and lived. Thus the Buddha strove hard to reach as far as his teacher in that doctrine so as ultimately "to dwell in the attainment of a knowledge and realisation thereof." He achieved success in his efforts "in no long time, but very speedily," whereupon his teacher, unable to contain himself, burst out as follows : "Happy, friend, are we ; yea, doubly happy, in that we look upon such a venerable one, such a fellow-ascetic as thee ! The doctrine which I know, that thou knowest : and the doctrine which thou knowest, that I know. As I am, so art thou ; as though art, so am I. Come, friend, you and I will together lead this company of ascetics." Thus did the teacher put his pupil "on a perfect level with himself, so honouring him with exceeding great honour." But Gautama, with whom there was no limit to spiritual development, could not remain satisfied with that doctrine. "Seeking the highest good, the incomparable path to Peace Supreme," he sought another teacher and "went where dwelt Uddaka, the disciple of Rāma, and thus addressed him : 'I wish, friend, to lead the ascetic life under this discipline and doctrine.' " As before, he "speedily acquired this doctrine so far as concerns lip-profession," and later on achieved sufficient mastery to be able "to abide in a realisation and knowledge of the doctrine," and was treated by his teacher as fully his equal ; but the full extent of this knowledge could not satisfy the soul of Gautama, ever yearning for the highest truth and still searching after the path of peace supreme. Thus Gautama had to part from both these teachers. It was a parting of Brāhmanical and Buddhist thought, fraught with profound consequences to the religious history of mankind. As Worsley well points out, "It is possible that, had Gautama chanced to meet, in his earliest wanderings, two teachers of the highest truth, the whole history of the old world might have been changed" [*Concepts of Monism*, p. 197]. But it is always to be remembered that the separation between Brāhmanism and Buddhism is not so complete as is often assumed. With the knowledge and training in Yoga received from his Brāhman masters, the Buddha now resolved to depend upon himself for his further progress, and retired to the jungles of Uruvelā near the present temple of Buddha-Gayā. There he "spied a beautiful secluded spot among the trees, with a pleasant, shallow, clear-flowing river close by, easily accessible, with fields and pastures all around," and immediately settled down, saying, "this suits well for effort." Early Buddhism, with its scheme of self-suppression, was not dead to the objective beauty of Nature as an aid to the inner, spiritual life.

Six years did Gautama spend in this life of self-education, the solitude of which was only relieved by the company of five Brahman ascetics, headed by Koṇḍañña, "the band of five elders," who, perceiving the promise of Buddhahood in him, attached themselves to him, "swept his cell, and did all manner of service for him, and kept constantly at his beck and call, all the time saying, 'Now he will become a Buddha, now he will become a Buddha.' "

His life at this stage is better described in his own words. Considering the homely illustration, that moist wood in water, or lying high up on the bank, cannot produce fire or flame, but only such as is dry and well-seasoned, he argued that Enlightenment could not come to one who was "not estranged from the body and from desires and, as concerns desires, is not inwardly rid of, has not wholly allayed sensual craving, weakness, thirst and fever." Thus he resolved to carry austerity to the uttermost, and tried various plans. First, with teeth clenched and tongue pressed to palate, he mastered, crushed and forced his mind into subjection. Second, he practised the Unbreathing Ecstasy, checking the ingoing and outgoing breath gradually in mouth and nose and ears. Thirdly, he tried to abstain from good, taking just a mouthful now and again of pottage made from beans, lentils, pulse or peas, till his body grew lean beyond measure, with his limbs like wasted, withered reeds, his backbone like a wavy rope, the gleam of his eye-balls far sunken, almost extinguished, the skin of his head hollow and shrunken like a served gourd uncooked and left out in the sun. "When I touched the surface of my stomach, my hand came into contact with my backbone, and when I felt at my backbone my hand encountered the skin of my stomach, and, going to attend to nature's calls, I toppled over for very weakness. When, somewhat to revive for fainting body, I stroked my limbs, lo! as I stroked, the hairs of my body rotted at the roots, came away in my hands, and all this by reason of the extremity of my abstention from food."

Apart from these austerities, a life of solitude was hard by itself. Gautama himself acknowledges that before he attained to full enlightenment he felt : "How hard to live the life of the lonely forest-dweller, away from men in solitary places ! How difficult to dwell aloof, to rejoice in solitude ! Verily, the silent groves must bear heavy upon the monk who has not won to fixity of mind !" He further describes how "all those ascetics and recluses who resort to hermitages far removed in the heart of the woods, while they are yet unpurified in deeds, words, thoughts, and manner of life, are seized with mortal fear and terror," to overcome which he would "go forth to the lonely tombs in the woods, out under the trees, and abide the night through in those places of horror and affright, so that he might know and experience that same fear and terror." Then he says : "And, as I tarried there, a deer came by, a bird caused a twig to fall, and the wind set all the leaves whispering ; and I thought : 'Now it is coming—that fear and terror !' And then I said within myself : 'But why should I stay still awaiting the certain coming of that fear ? How if, as soon as that fear and terror takes shape and form, I meet and master the oncoming fear and terror !' And that fear and terror came as I walked to and fro ; but I neither stood still, nor sat, nor lay down until, pacing to and fro, I had mastered that fear and terror. And that fear and terror came over me as I stood still, or sat, or lay down, but I neither sat up nor stood up, nor paced

THE BUDDHA (SARNATH)

to and fro until lying down, I had mastered that fear and terror."

There is another description of his ascetic life, of which he practised all the four kinds, viz.: (*a*) *Rigorous* as regards food and clothing; (*b*) *Offensive*, allowing dirt to accumulate on the body; (*c*) *Scrupulous*, *e.g.* as regards the life of tiny creatures swarming in a drop of water; and (*d*) *Solitary*, "fleeing from grove to grove, thicket to thicket, glen to glen, hill to hill, at the sight of a cowherd, or a goatherd, a grass-gatherer, a faggot-gatherer or a forester" [*Maj. N.*].

The practice of these penances, which, as Gautama justly supposed, had beaten all record [*Maj. N.*, tr., p. 105, vol. ii.] only left him physically weak and spiritually unsatisfied. He thought: "With all these bitter austerities, I do not reach aught beyond the human, do not attain to any sufficing pre-eminence of exalted knowledge and insight; might there be some other way to Enlightenment?" [*ibid.*]. He further considered: "It were not easy to attain to this blessedness with body so exceedingly lean and wasted; how if I eat of substantial food and rice porridge?" And he accordingly "began to partake of solid food and rice porridge. On this the five monks about him, who were serving him in the hope that, when he should attain to truth, he would impart it to them, now deserted him in disgust, saying one to another: "The Ascetic Gotama has become luxurious; he has ceased from striving and turned to a life of comfort". They even deserted the place too and made off to Isipatana in Benares.

Thus putting an end to this course of self-mortification, the Bodhisattva began begging for his food, and came to the foot of a tree on the full-moon day of the month Vaiśākha, when it was time for Sujātā, the chieftain's daughter, to offer worship to the tree. With her maid Puṇṇā, she brought an offering of milk-rice cooked in a golden dish, and, supposing the Buddha to be the tree-god, gave it to him. Taking the dish, he went up to the banks of the Nerañjarā river, bathed at a place called *Supatiṭṭhita*, made the whole of the thick, sweet milk-rice into forty-nine portions, and ate the whole food, resolving not to take any nourishment during the next seven weeks. Taking his noon-day rest on the banks of the river in a grove of sāl trees in full bloom, he went in the evening towards a Bo-tree, meeting on the way a grass-cutter named Sotthiya (Svastika), who gave him eight bundles of grass to serve as his seat. He sat cross-legged under the tree, facing the east, and took the following vow : "Let my skin, my nerves and bones waste away ; let all the flesh and blood in my body dry up, but never from this seat will I stir until I have attained the supreme and absolute wisdom ! " Thus during all this time he neither ate "nor bathed, nor rinsed his mouth, nor did he ease himself," but gave himself completely to meditation (jhāna=dhyāna), which could not be disturbed even by "the descent of a hundred thunderbolts at once." On the very first day of this meditation, at the age of thirty-five, Gautama attained to Enlightenment or became the *Buddha*. But he kept to his seat under the Bo-tree for seven days "experiencing the bliss of emancipation." Three more weeks he spent near the Bodhi tree. In the fifth week he moved towards the Goat-herd's (Ajapāla) banyan tree, in the sixth week to the Muchalinda tree, in the seventh to the Rājāyatana tree, at the foot of which, on the last day of the seventh week, he was offered cakes of barley and honey as food by two merchants, Tapussa and Bhallika, who came there in the course of their travelling with 500 carts from Utkala to Madhyadeśa. After the Buddha had finished his meal, they prostrated themselves before him, saying: "We take refuge in the Buddha and the Law: take us, O Lord, from henceforward lifelong as lay-devotees." Thus these two were the first converts, though only lay converts, of the Buddha.

But presently there was a reaction in the Buddha's mind as regards preaching of his faith. Returning to the Ajāpala tree, he considered that the Truth he has won was too "profound and subtle" for "this race of mankind, who only seek and revel in pleasure," and thought : "Should I publish this teaching abroad and others fail to understand, it would only result in trouble and vexation for me." But soon a more tolerant view dawned on him, when he perceived that the world was full of beings of all kinds, and not merely of the "impure, bad, dull and stupid," "like a tank showing various lotuses, red, white or blue, submerged or rising from the water." He finally uttered his decision thus : "Of deathlessness, lo! I disclose the portals. Ye that have ears come, hearken and believe !" The ascetics and teachers of ancient India were not anti-social or self-centred : they renounced the world only to be able to serve it better with their capacities improved by that life of renunciation. The solitary seeker of Truth must end as a teacher of Truth and invite others to a participation of the spiritual treasures which he does not treat as his individual, but common, property.

Thus ends his life of renunciation, followed by a life of active social service, in the highest sense, for forty-five years, from the age of thirty-five to his death at eighty. The history of this ministry is the history of the spread of Buddhism, which, from a local sect, grew to be one of the world-religions within a few centuries.

The course of the new faith did not run smooth at first. The Buddha, with his natural, nay, supernatural, nobility, thought of making his first teachers his first disciples too, to share with them the Truths which they alone, thought he, as being "learned and free from all defilement," would "most speedily apprehend." That was the highest honour which their whilom pupil could pay to his teachers ! But, unfortunately, both Āḷāra Kālāma and Uddaka were no longer in the land of the living. Next, the Buddha naturally thought of his other early associates, the five ascetics who had deserted him in distrust, and retired to the

Deer-park of Isipatana at Benares, the centre of Brāhmanism, as the fittest persons to receive his teaching. Thus his steps were led towards Benares in a fateful march, fraught with profound consequences to the religious history of humanity. "On the way, between the Bodhi tree and Gayā, Upaka, the naked ascetic, met him and addressed him thus : 'Placid and serene is thy countenance, friend, thy skin clear and bright. Under whom have you taken your vows : what is your Teacher's name : whose is the doctrine which you profess ?' The Buddha answered that, renouncing all, he was self-taught. The cynical Upaka said : 'It may be so, friend ; it may be so,' and, nodding his head and turning into a side road, he went on his way." This was one of the very few instances of scepticism which the Buddha confronted and failed to convince.

In the evening, he arrived at the Deer-park of Benares in search of his five earlier associates, who had lost faith in him for his backsliding, as they took it. Thus they were the worst persons to be taught by the Buddha. And the Buddha too deliberately proposed to try his teaching first on them, to make his pronounced detractors his first disciples, so that the triumph of his doctrine might be the greater. They are courteous enough to give him a seat and a hearing, which thus occasions the Buddha's first sermon and sets rolling the wheel of Buddhism (Dharma-chakra-pravartana). The sermon was naturally meant to solve the doubts of his audience regarding the

4

virtues of self-indulgence and self-mortification, both of which the Buddha condemned as extremes to be replaced by the Middle Path, made up of the following eight elements:

1. Right Views.
2. Right Resolve.
3. Right Speech.
4. Right Action.
5. Right Living.
6. Right Effort.
7. Right Recollectedness.
8. Right Meditation.

This 'Noble Eightfold Path' was suggested by the 'Four Noble Truths' (ārya-satyāni), which were explained as Sorrow, the Cause of Sorrow, the Cessation of Sorrow and the Path Leading to the Cessation of Sorrow.[1]

---

[1] The Buddha's first sermon indicates the foundations of Buddhism. It is not a teaching of pessimism, but of emancipation. The fact of evil or sorrow is to be recognised only to get over it. Without evil there is no thought about emancipation, which a happy world won't need. The objection that Buddhism seeks to remove the evil of life by removing life itself is answered by the Eightfold Path, which will be acceptable to the modern worlds as a practical scheme of the good life, as compared with the paths to salvation proposed by other Indian schools, such as the Brāhamanical ceremonies, or the courses of penance and self-mortification or philosophical discussions associated with the six Tīrthikas. The Buddha's Eightfold Path is not exclusively external and practical, considering the items 2 and 7 ; nor does it ignore the will, for the items 4, 5, and 6 show that Buddhism is not a dreamy, subjective, unpractical religion.

The discourse had its immediate effect upon their leader Koṇḍañña (Kauṇḍiṇya), who came to true insight at once. The next day was converted Vappa (Vāṣpa), and on the three following days Bhaddiya (Bhadrika), Mahānāman and Assaji (Aśvajit) successively.) The Buddha initiated them in the following words: "Come near, O Monks; well-preached is the doctrine! walk in purity to make an end of all suffering." Thus the five founded the Buddhist Saṅgha. On the fifth day the Buddha delivered to them a second discourse "on the instability and impermanence of everything earthly" (Anattalakkhaṇa-Suttanta), by comprehending which the five monks became perfectly enlightened. "At this time," as the story states, "there were six holy persons in the world"—these five and the Buddha.

The number of his followers now begins to swell. The first five were recruited from religious orders. But now recruits were coming in from secular classes. Yasa, the son of a wealthy banker of Benares, tired of worldly life, goes to the Deer-park and receives the Buddha's teaching. His example is followed by his parents and wife, who become lay-devotees, and by fifty-four friends of

---

Item 8 promises fulfilment—the beatific vision—in this life to the persevering devotee. "The negative features of the Path are also important. It contains no mention of ceremonial, austerities, gods, many or one, nor of the Buddha himself. He is the discoverer and teacher of the truth: beyond that his personality plays no part" [Eliot, *Hinduism and Buddhism*, i. 145].

his, youths from aristocratic families, so as to bring the total number of his disciples to sixty. Then at the end of the rainy season, five months after his attainment of Enlightenment under the Bo-tree, and three months after his arrival at the Deer-park, the Buddha assembled his sixty disciples, and said: "Go ye out, O disciples, and travel from place to place for the welfare and joy of many people. Go not in twos to one place. Preach the Law in spirit and in letter, the whole and full, pure path of holiness."

For his own part, he preferred to retrace his steps to the village of the general (Sena), Uruvelā, a stronghold of Brāhmanism, where lived 1000 Jaṭilas with their three leaders, the brothers, Uruvelā, Nadī and Gayā of the Kassapa family. They presently with all their followers yielded to the power and superiority of the Buddha, as he delivered his third discourse on Fire (the Fire of Desire) on the hill of Gayāśīrṣa. The next move was to the bamboo-thicket (Yaṣṭivana) outside Rājagriha, where the Buddha with his new disciples was visited by King Bimbisāra with a large following of citizens and Brāhmans, whose doubts as to whether the renowned Brāhman Kassapa was the teacher or pupil of Gautama were set at rest by the former openly declaring himself as the disciple. The Buddha then preached before the king, who with many of his retinue became a lay-devotee. Before taking leave the king invited the Buddha and his Order to meals the next day at his palace at Rājagṛiha.

The king with his own hands served the food, and at the conclusion of the dinner made a gift to the Saṅgha of the Bamboo Grove (Veluvana) near the city.

While at Rājagṛiha, the Buddha secured as his disciples the Brāhmans Sāriputta and Moggallāna, who were among the 250 followers of the paribbājaka Sañjaya. Sāriputta was drawn towards the Buddha by the effects of his teaching which he perceived in his pupil Assaji, whose luminous face impressed him as he was once going through the city on his begging rounds.

The dissolution and conversion of the Order of Sajñajya, followed as they were by numerous other conversions of "many distinguished and noble youths of the Magadha territory," created quite a sensation and some amount of uneasiness among the people, who murmured that "the ascetic Gotama is come to bring childlessness, widowhood and subversion of families." The Buddha's answer to the complaint was that he was converting people only by the power of truth.

From Rājagṛiha he went for a time to Benares, where he spent the time of Retreat during the rains, and then came back to Uruvelā, whence, after a stay of three months, he went to Rājagṛiha, where envoys after envoys were coming to him from his father with instructions to bring him to Kapilavastu. But each time they remained to be converted by the Buddha and failed to deliver to him the king's message. This happened nine times, till an old playmate of his,

Udāyin by name, was deputed by the king. Though he also became a monk and an Arhat under the master's teaching, he was careful to deliver the king's message when the time was favourable for travelling at the end of the cold season and advent of spring. The Tathāgata agreed to go to Kapilavastu, which he reached in about two months.

The Buddha stopped at the Banyan (Nyagrodha) Grove outside the city, where he was visited by his father and other kinsmen, who omitted to provide for the meals of the Buddha and his Order. Thus the next day he set out early with his disciples on his begging rounds through the city. This put to shame his royal father, who remonstrated that such conduct was unworthy of his race. The Buddha replied: "Yours, O King, is the lineage of Kings, but mine is that of the Buddhas, who have always lived on alms." Then he utters a moving verse, which converts his father, who next leads the Buddha and his Order to the palace, where they were treated to a savoury meal. After the meal the ladies of the palace came to pay respects to the Buddha, except his sensitive wife, to whose private apartments he went himself, and then she threw herself at her Lord's feet. On the second day, which was fixed for the inauguration of his cousin Nanda (son of his stepmother Gotamī) as crown prince and for his marriage to Janapada-Kalyāṇī, a noted beauty of the land, the strange event happened of the Buddha taking away Nanda to the Banyan garden and making him embrace monkhood there. On the seventh day, the mother of Rāhula asked him, as the rightful heir of the Buddha, to claim his paternal inheritance. The Buddha answered that claim by asking Sāriputta to confer on Rāhula the novice ordination (pabbajjā), so that he might be the heir of the spiritual inheritance owned by his father. The monkhood of Rāhula, following that of Gotama and of Nanda, deprived Śuddhodana of all possible male heirs to his kingdom, besides causing him "great pain"; for "the love for a son, Lord," as he himself put it, "cuts into the skin, the flesh, the bones, and reaches the marrow." His grievance was met by the Buddha making the rule that no one should be admitted to the Order without the consent of his parents.

From Kapilavastu the master went to Anupiya on the Anomā in the Malla country, where he converted Ānanda, his most intimate disciple, Devadatta, his obstinate opponent, Upāli, the barber who became afterwards a noted leader of the Order, and Anuruddha, the master of Buddhist metaphysics.

The next move was to Rājagṛiha, where the Buddha stayed at the Sītavana and converted the merchant Sudatta, surnamed Anāthapiṇḍika, a native of Śrāvastī. With the zeal of a new covert, that merchant-prince returned to his native city, where he invited the Buddha to spend his next rainy season or retreat, and proposed to buy of Prince Jeta, for the master and Order, his beautiful Jetavana Park near the city. But the prince said : "It is not, sir, for sale even for a sum so great that the pieces of money would be sufficient to cover it, if they were laid side by side." The merchant said: "I take, sir, the garden at that price." The prince, puzzled, answered: "No, O householder, there was no bargain meant." But the merchant pursued the matter like an unrelenting Shylock (though for a far different purpose), sued the prince for non-fulfilment of contract and obtained a favourable decision of the court, which declared: "The Ārāma, sir, is taken at the price which you fixed." Then he had crores of gold pieces brought, as many as, being laid side by side, could cover up the entire ground of the garden. There he also erected a splendid Vihāra or monastery with a private room (gandhakuṭī) for the master in the centre and separate dwelling rooms and cells for the monks. Then he invited the Buddha, received him right royally, and with his permission made a formal gift of the Vihāra to the "Saṅgha present and future" [*Chulla Vagga*, vi. 4].

Śrāvastī, which was then the capital of King Prasenajit of Kosala, brought to the Order the distinguished lady recruit, Viśākhā, the wife of Pūrnavardhana, son of the rich merchant Migāra. As the benefactress of the church, she made a gift of the monastery of Pūrvārāma, only second in splendour to the Jetavana Vihāra. It was a "storeyed building (prāsāda) with a verandah to it supported on pillars with capitals shaped like elephant heads."

The narrative of the Buddha's life, as given in the Pāli Jātaka book and the Sanskrit *Mahāvastu* and *Lalita-Vistara*, is not carried beyond this incident of his visit to Śrāvastī. It is given for the few days before his death in the *Mahāparinirbāṇa Sūtra*. The incidents of the interval can only be roughly gathered from the details recorded of the time, place and circumstances in which the Buddha delivered his different sermons during a ministy of over 40 years.

A useful accession to the Order was the most renowned physician of the times, Jīvaka, surnamed Komārabhachcha, for his special proficiency in the treatment of children's diseases. Prince Abhaya, son of King Bimbisāra, brought him up and sent him to Taxilā for medical studies. After seven years' study he became an expert, with his practice extending from Śrāvastī to Ujjayinī over several kingdoms, including cities like Benares and Vaiśālī between. King Bimbisāra, who made him his physician in ordinary, also attached him to the Buddha and his Order. Once the Buddha fell ill of constipation. Jīvaka attended on him, and first prescribed fat, with which Ānanda rubbed his body for a few days, and then, finding that to be not effective, prescribed a mild purgative, comprising three handfuls of three lotuses imbued with drugs which were to be smelt by the patient. This prescription proving effective, the Buddha was asked to bathe in warm water and abstain from liquid food for some time. Jīvaka served the Buddha most devotedly, and once gave him some very rich cloth with which King Pradyotaof Ujjayinī had rewarded his skill.

The chronicle of his ministry, as worked out by Dr. Rhys Davids, shows that the first retreat or rainy season was spent at Benares and the next three at Rājagṛiha in the Bamboo grove. A deputation from Vaiśālī waited on him for his visit to the city to purge it of the frightful plague then raging there. Thus was made his first visit to that republican city, of which the Lichchhavi nobles gave him a royal reception on the other side of the river Gaṅgā.

The visit to Vaiśālī was repeated in the fifth rainy season spent at the Kūṭāgāra hall of the Mahāvana grove. From there he twice visited Kapilavastu, first, to prevent what threatened to be a bloody dispute between the Sākyas and Koliyas regarding the waters of the Rohiṇī in a season of drought and, secondly, to perform his last duties by his father dying at 97. He then returns to Vaiśālī, but is followed there by his foster-mother Prajāpatī, his wife Yaśodharā and several other Śākya and Koliyan ladies who wanted to embrace the monastic life. At first unwilling to comply with their wishes, the Buddha yielded to the advocacy of Ānanda (one of the very rare occasions when he yields to argument) and instituted a separate Order of Nuns for them with its own rules and regulations. But the Buddha was careful to point out that but for this concession to women, now declared eligible for the Order, "the pure religion would have lasted long, the good law would have stood fast for a thousand years. But now it will last for only 500 years" [*Maha. Par. Sutta*, v. 23].

From Vaiśālī a move is made to the hill Makula at Kauśāmbī near Allahabad, where is spent the sixth retreat or rainy season.

Then he again returned to Rājagṛiha, where Kṣemā, the proud queen of Bimbisāra, had her pride humbled and was admitted to the Order. One of his disciples also humbled the pride of the six chiefs of non-Buddhist sects by a display of superhuman powers, for which he is rebuked by the Buddha, who henceforth prohibits such practices, saying, "This will not conduce either to the conversion of the unconverted or to the advantage of the converted."

The seventh retreat is passed at Śrāvastī, where his opponent teachers tried to destroy his reputation by foul means. They secured a woman, Chiñchā by name, dressed up artificially like a pregnant woman, to accuse him of having intercourse with her, but the artifice was at once exposed.

The eighth retreat was held at the Crocodile hill in the Deer-park of the Bhesakalā forest in the Bharga country. The Buddha and his Order were asked to dinner at a newly completed palace by Prince Bodhi, who had the whole building down to the last row of steps covered over with white cloth as a decoration. But the Buddha would not tread on the cloth, as being inadmissible for monks, and so the cloth had to be removed.

The ninth retreat is passed at Kauśāmbī in the Vihāra called Ghoṣitārāma, presented by Ghoṣita, one of the three ministers of King Udayana of the Vatsa country. Here a controversy on a small point of discipline between two monks developed into a regular division in the brotherhood, which even the Buddha's repeated exhortations failed to check, whereupon, feeling that he had had enough of society and disciples, he withdrew himself to the forest of Pārileyyaka after meeting on the way the hermit Bhagu in a village, and Anuruddha and two other hermits at the Pāchīnavamsadāya or Eastern Bamboo wood. There he very much enjoyed the solitary life, like a lonely elephant living away from the herd.

Then he returns to Śrāvastī to spend there his tenth retreat. In the meanwhile the rebellious monks of Kauśāmbī, losing by their behaviour the support of that city, now seek out their master in repentance.

The eleventh retreat is passed at Rājagṛiha, where the Brāhman Bhāradvāja, who ploughed and sowed for his livelihood, was converted by the parable of the sower presented as follows: "Faith is the seed, devotion the rain, modesty the ploughshaft, the mind the tie of the yoke, mindfulness the ploughshare and goad, truthfulness the means to bind, tenderness to untie, and energy the team and bullock."

The twelth rainy season is spent at Verañjā, after which the Buddha makes his longest journey as far as Soreyya near Taxilā; thence to Sāṅkaśya, Kanouj, Prayag, where he crossed the Gaṅgā on his way to Benares, whence again he comes to Vaiśālī and stops at the Kūṭāgāra hall.

The thirteenth retreat was spent at Chālikā and Srāvastī, and at the latter place, the fourteenth retreat too, during which his son Rāhula at 20 was ordained.

The fifteenth retreat was also spent at Śrāvastī, but in the Nyagrodha grove. It is associated with two events: (1) the addressing of a discourse by the Buddha to his cousin Mahānāman when he became head of the Śākya clan in succession to Bhaddiya, who succeeded his father Śuddhodana; (2) the cursing of the Buddha by his father-in-law, Suprabuddha, for his desertion of his daughter.

The seventeenth season is spent at Rājagṛiha, the eighteenth at Chālikā, the nineteenth in the Veluvana at Rājagṛiha, and the twentieth in the Jetavana at Śrāvastī, where he appoints Ānanda to be his personal attendant in place of another mendicant who had twice insulted him in carrying his alms-bowl. At this time, in a forest near, Chālikā, he faces the famous robber Aṅgulimāla subdues his evil nature and persuades him to become a monk. In a short time the robber attains to the perfection of an Arhat.

His stay at the Jetavana was marked by two incidents. An attempt was made by his opponents to destroy his reputation by bringing about the death of the nun Sundarī through hired assassins, and throwing away her corpse near the

Vihāra, attributing the crime to the Buddha. The plot was however soon discovered, to the shame of the culprits. The second incident arose out of the marriage of Anāthapiṇḍika's daughter, Subhadrā, to the son of a friend of his in Aṅga, a follower of the naked ascetics. The girl's faith in the Buddha was being put to the severest tests, which led the Buddha with 500 disciples to proceed to Aṅga, where his preaching converted the whole family. He returned to Śrāvastī after leaving Anuruddha to complete the work of conversion begun in Aṅga. The Soṇadaṇḍa Sutta mentions the Blessed One "going on a tour through the Aṅga country with about 500 brethren" and stopping for some time at Champā.

The chronicle of the ministry again breaks off at the twentieth year, to be resumed towards the close of Buddha's life. Two important episodes are connected with the interval. His cousin Devadatta proposed that the Buddha, by reason of age (he was then 72), should retire in his favour from the leadership of the Order. The Buddha thrice refusing that request, Devadatta became his declared enemy and was 'proclaimed' as such publicly by Śāriputra and other monks at Rājagṛiha under the Buddha's orders. The exasperated Devadatta now leagued himself with Ajātaśatru, first, to remove from the throne the latter's father Bimbisāra, the patron and protector of Buddhism, and, secondly, to put the Buddha out of the way and take his place. The first part of this nefarious design succeeded by Bimbisāra's abdication or murder[1] by his son. The second part failed miserably. Three attempts on the life of the Buddha were made by Devadatta. At last he tried to injure him by stirring up discord in the Order. He got up a party of some monks to represent to him that the rules should be stricter as regards food, clothing and shelter. The Buddha, while approving of strictness, refused to make it obligatory on all monks, and thus gave Devadatta an opportunity to pose as an uncompromising Puritan and thereby to gather a large following of 500 Vṛijiaṅ monks, new to the Order, whose ignorance was thus fully exploited. With them he settled at the Gayāśīrṣa hill near Rājagṛiha. One night, while addressing the Assembly, he noticed Śāriputra and Maudgalyāyana among them, and, believing that they were deserters from the Buddha, and himself feeling sleepy, while the Assembly was eager for a sermon, he asked them to address the Assembly in his place. The result of their address was that the 500 schismatics returned to the Buddha's Order. The Buddha's victory was also achieved in the other direction. Ajātasatru, stung by remorse for his sin, sought consolation in vain from the six Tīrthikas, and was advised by the physician Jīvaka to go to the spiritual physician, the Buddha, instead. The result of the interview was his conversion to the new faith. The other episode was the destruction of his own native city,

[1] In the *Dig. Nik.* ii. the Buddha himself says that Ajātaśatru "put his father to death."

Kapilavastu, and his own people, the Śākyas, by Viḍūḍabha, son of Prasenajit, in his wrath at the discovery of an early fraud by the Śākyas, who passed off a low-born woman, now his mother, as one of pure Śākya blood. The Budha lived to see these sorrowful occurrences.

We now come to the account of the last stage of his life. During his 79th year, when he was sojourning on the Gṛidhrakūṭa near Rājagṛiha, Ajātaśatru wanted to invade Vaiśālī, and asked for the Buddha's opinion on his project. The Buddha declared that so long as the Vṛijians lived in harmony they would be invincible.[1]

Then the master travelled with Ānanda to a number of places: Ambalaṭṭhikā, Nālandā (staying at the Pāvārika Mango grove), Pāṭaligrāma, where Ajātaśatru was having a fort[2] built against

---

[1] According to the *Mahā Parinibbāṇa Sutta*, the Buddha's opinion on the project was asked by the king through his Prime Minister, the Brāhman Vassakāra, to whom the Buddha explained that the Vajjians were not to decline, but to prosper, so long as they conformed to the following conditions, viz. (*a*) holding and frequenting the public meetings of their clan; (*b*) unity in deliberation and administration; (*c*) honouring their ancient institutions; (*d*) showing the respect due to their elders; (*e*) supporting the old shrines with continuance of the proper offering and rites as formerly given and performed; (*f*) honouring the Arahants among them.

[2] The fort was being built by the chief ministers of Magadha, Sunīdha and Vassakāra, who gave themselves the honour of giving a dinner to the Buddha at their house, and instituted the Gotama gate and Gotama ferry

the Lichchhavi menace on the other side of the river —the beginning of what the Buddha prophesied would be the great city of Pāṭaliputra. Here the Buddha crossed the Ganges and went on to Koṭigrāma, Nādikā (where he stayed in the *Brick Hall*), and to Vaiśālī, where an invitation was extended to him by the hospitable courtesan Ambapālī in anticipation of the Lichchhavi noblemen, who could not buy her off her engagement even "for a hundred thousand." Her firm reply was : "My lords, were you to offer all Vesālī with its subject territory, I would not give up so honourable a feast." The dinner was followed by her gift to the Order of her beautiful mango grove.

From Vaiśālī the master moved on to a village, Beluva, close by, where he spent his last retreat, and had a severe attack of illness, during which he prophesied : "At the end of 3 months hence the Tathāgata will die." After recovery he came back to his favourite Kūṭāgāra hall in the Mahāvana at Vaiśālī, whence he went to Pāvā, staying at the Mango grove of Chunda the smith. The smith treated him to a meal of rice and mushroom (not 'pork,' as is often stated), which brought o an attack of dysentery while he was half-way o

at the places at which the Buddha went out of the city and crossed the river respectively. The greatness of th city was thus foretold by him : "As far as Āryan peop resort, as far as merchants travel, this will become t chief city, Pāṭaliputra, a centre for the interchange of kinds of wares" [*Maha. P. Sutta*].

the road to Kusinārā. Too weak tc travel, he asked Ānanda for drinking water from the river Kukutthā close by, which temporarily restored him and enabled him to reach a grove outside the city of his destination, where he rested for the last time, spending his last hours in imparting useful instructions and counsels to Ānanda. A couch was spread by Ānanda between two Sāl trees, on which he placed his head to the north and laid himself down on his right side with one leg resting on the other. Even in his last hour he converted the Brāhman philosopher, Subhadra, whom Ānanda would not admit to his presence because of his illness. But the master woud not deny himself to a seeker of truth even in his dying moment ! Then for the last time he called his monks together and asked them whether any one had any doubts on any point in his teachings, "that ye may not later regret not having asked me whilst I yet tarried among you." The monks remained silent, and then he addressed them a final exhortation, with the following as his last words : "Now, monks, I have nothing more to tell you than this : decay is inherent in all compounded things. Work out your salvation energetically."

Thus closed the life of one who lived to achieve the highest wisdom and purity among mortals and was also the most active in their service, to which he dedicated the best part of his long life.

In conclusion, we may note some of the chief features of his life and character.

The scene of his ministry of 45 years was laid largely in the eastern part of India, of which the two extreme points were the cities of Śrāvasti and Rājagṛiha. Only once is he reported to have travelled beyond these limits. Between these two cities, along the road which the Buddha used, there lay many intermediate places associated with his ministry; such as Nālandā, Pāṭaliputta, Vesālī, Bhaṇḍagāma, Pāvā, Kusinārā, Kapilavatthu, Setavya with Benares and Kosambī. A passage in the *Majjhima Nikāya* refers to the Blessed One also tarrying "in the land of the Kurus, at a Kuru town named Kammāssadhammam," and another in the *Dīgha Nikaya* to his sojourning in Aṅga. The sphere of his ministry, the home of ancient Buddhism, thus embraced the territory not of a single state, but of several kingdoms, as well as republics. The Buddha's pilgrim-life was spent in the kingdoms of Kośala, Kāśī, Magadha, and in the republican territories of the Śākyas and Malas, the Vṛijians and Lichchhavis, and, towards the north-west, in the lands of "the Cheṭis and Vaṃsas, the Kurus and Pañchālas, the Machchhas and Sūrasenas" [Jana-Vasabha Suttanta], all of which owned a common subjection to the spiritual sovereignty and empire he was gradually building up. At each of the places of preaching, the places of his retreat during the rains, the piety of devotees provided for the residence of the master and his Order. Thus at Rājagṛiha he would reside in the Veluvana or Yaṣṭivana or the Uruvelā village; at Śrāvastī there was the famous Jetavana and its elaborately constructed Vihāra, as well as the Pubbārāma; at Kauśāmbī, he had the Ghositārāma at his disposal; Vaiśālī is noted for its Mahāvana with its Kūṭāgāra hall, and for his second residence at the Mango grove of Āmrapālī; at Pāvā he would stay in Chunda's mango grove and later in the new mote-hall named Ubbhaṭaka built by the Mallas who had it formally opened by the Buddha [Saṅgīti Suttanta]; Kapilavastu had its Nyagrodha grove, and Benaras its deer-park at Isipatana. These are some of the holy places of Buddhism, being associated with the preachings of its founder.

The very extent of the range of his ministry proves how active must have been his daily life uniformly for a period of 45 years. A graphic picture of his daily life and the environment in which it was lived is drawn by Buddhaghosa. "He rose early in the morning (*i.e.* about 5 a.m.), and, out of consideration for his personal attendant, was wont to wash and dress himself, without calling for any assistance. Then, till it was time to go on his round for alms, he would retire to a solitary place and meditate. When that time arrived,[1] he would dress himself completely in the three robes, take his bowl in his hand and, sometimes alone and sometimes attended by his

[1] Not unfrequently it is found that even after his morning meditation was over it was too early to set out on his begging round, and then he would use that interval by visiting some good monk of the neighbourhood.

followers, would enter the neighbouring village or town for alms. Then the people, understanding that 'to-day it is the Blessed One has come for alms,' would vie with one another, saying: 'To-day, Sir, take your meal with us; we will make provision for ten, and we for twenty, and we for a hundred of your followers.' So saying, they would take his bowl and, spreading mats for him and his attendant followers, would await the moment when the meal was over. Then would the Blessed One, when the meal was done, discourse to them, with due regard to their capacity for spiritual things, in such a way that some would take the layman's vow, and some would enter on the paths, and some would reach the highest truth thereof. This done, he would arise from his seat and depart for the place where he had lodged. And when he had come there, he would sit in the open verandah, awaiting the time when the rest of his followers should also have finished their meal. And when his attendant announced they had done so, he would enter his private apartment. Thus was he occupied up to the mid-day meal. Then afterwards, standing at the door of his chamber, he would exhort the congregation of brethren into strenuous efforts after the higher life. Then would some of them ask him to suggest a subject for meditation suitable to the special capacity of each, and when he had done so, they would retire each to the solitary place he was wont to frequent, and meditate on the subject set. Then would the

Blessed One retire within the private chamber for short rest during the heat of the day.[1] Then when his body was rested, he would arise from the couch and for a space consider the circumstances of the people near him that he might do them good. And at the fall of the day the folk from the neighbouring villages or town would gather together at the place where he was lodging, and to them seated in the lecture-hall would he, in a manner suitable to the occasion and to their beliefs, discourse on the truth. Then, seeing that the proper time had come, he would dismiss the folk. Thus was he occupied in the afternoon. Then at close of the day, should he feel a need of the refreshment of a bath, he would bathe, the while some brother of the Order attendant on him would prepare the divan in the chamber perfumed with flowers. And in the evening he would sit a while alone, still in all his robes, till the brethren returned from their meditations began to assemble. Then some would ask him questions on things that puzzled them, some would speak of their meditations, some would ask for an exposition of the truth. Thus would the first watch of the night pass, as the Blessed One satisfied the desire of each, and then they would take their leave. And part

[1] On one occasion at this hour he retired to a wood with his son Rāhula to impart to him some instruction, but as a rule he did not give further instruction until the late afternoon [*Maj. N.* 147]. He would also on occasions be 'meditating during the noon-day heat" [*Sam. N.* i. 146-148].

of the rest of the night would he spend in meditation, walking up and down outside his chamber, and part he would rest, laying down, calm and self-possessed, within" [adapted from translation in Dr. Rhys Davids' *American Lectures*].

Thus the round of his daily activities comprised meditation, begging for alms, or attending invitations for meals, followed by discourse to the laity, leading to fresh conversions, return to the monastery, suggestion of subjects for meditation by the monks in their chambers after midday meal, his own retirement for meditation, discourse to the public in the afternoon, evening bath, meditation, discourse with monks after meditation, meditation and rest. His was thus a double life—the *inner* life of introspection and meditation and the *outer* life of objective activity, consecrated to the service of his fellow human beings—like the two wings of a bird by which it is upborne in its progress towards the skies!

The language in which the Buddha preached to the people was not Sanskrit, but what was then the popular idiom of Eastern Hindustan, allied to Pāli. But he permitted every disciple to learn his words in his own mother-tongue.

The Buddha held his congregations with perfect mastery. Believers addressed him as Bhagavā, or Bhante, Lord. Visitors "bowed to him or exchanged with him the greetings and compliments of politeness and courtesy" and then took their seats on one side. Some would call out their name and family before taking seats. When the meeting was over, the audience rose from their seats, 'bowed down before the Blessed One, and walking round him with his right hand towards him departed thence."

Sometimes the congregations were continued to a late hour at night. The *Majjhima Nikāya* (110), for instance, refers to an assembly held in the light of the full moon with the Buddha sitting in perfect silence, which was only broken by a monk putting a question, rising, adjusting his robe so as to leave one shoulder bare, and make a bow with his hands joined and raised to his forehead. Then the Buddha would tenderly say: "Be seated, monk, ask what you will." When the Emperor Ajātaśatru went to see the Buddha in the mango grove of Jīvaka at the latter's advice (and against that of his six other ministers, who advised him to see the six Tīrthikas instead) on a full moon night, he was seized with a sudden fear at the unearthly silence, and, suspecting an ambush, said to Jīvaka: "You are playing me no tricks, Jīvaka? You are not betraying me to my foes? How can it be that there should be no sound at all, not a sneeze, nor a cough, in so large an assembly, among 1250 of the brethren?" Jīvaka assured him that there was no mischief afoot: "Go on, O king, go straight on. There in the pavilion hall the lamps are burning, and that is the Blessed One sitting against the middle pillar, facing the east, with the brethren around him." And, when the king looked on the assembly seated in perfect silence, calm as a clear lake, he broke out: "Would that my son Udāyi Bhadda might have such calm as this assembly of the brethren now has!" [*Dī. N.* ii.].

The style of his discourse, as preserved in the Pāli works, was similar to what we find in the discourses of the older Vedic literature like the Upaniṣads, with its absence of any warmth or passion, its severe dignity, its sublime uniformity, and its burden of schematic repetitions, leaving no scope for any flight of fancy. "There is no impassioned entreating of men to come to his faith; no bitterness for the unbelieving who remain afar off." Sometimes, instead of a sermon, we find a dialogue. The Buddha is questioned and he puts a counter-question. Sometimes parables alternate with doctrine and didactic discourse. He employs similes drawn from the life of man and the life of nature, of which he was such a keen observer. From similes there is sometimes a natural transition to fable and romance. Sometimes, again, where he gives expression to the simple emotions, hopes and fears, joys and sorrows of the ordinary, universal human heart, his discourse reaches high levels of poetry, but its ruling characteristic is its severity, its austere dignity. "The living human, the personal, hides itself behind the system, the formula. There is no one to seek out and to console the suffering and the sorrowing. It is only the sorrow of the whole creation of which we again and again hear."

A characteristic feature of his method in debate was to put and examine his opponent's position first. Nigrodha the wanderer, who had a following of 3000, thought about the Buddha, that by his habit of seclusion "his insight was ruined, he is not at home in conducting an assembly, nor ready in conversation, but occupied only with the fringes of things," and to prove the truth of his opinion asked the Buddha to expound his doctrine. The Buddha, not to be outwitted, said: "Difficult is it, Nigrodha, for one of another view, without practice or teaching, to understand that wherein I train my disciples," and, turning the tables thus, said: "Come now, Nigrodha, ask me a question about your own doctrine." Upon this, his followers shouted out: "Wonderful, Sir, the great gifts and powers of the Samaṇa Gotama in withholding his own theories and inviting the discussion of those of others!" Thus, by way of criticising his opponent's doctrine, he established his own, after which the wanderers said: "Herein are we and our teachers set at naught" and "sat silent and annoyed, with hunched back and drooping head, brooding and dumbfounded." Their leader confessed his offence, and promised to restrain himself in future.

Only, very rarely, under some deep provocation due to the heresy of any of the brethren, does a stray gleam of emotion break through his accustomed severity: "Perverted of understanding, witless one, thou seekest to correct us and diggest thine own grave, and heapest up guilt for thyself. For long, foolish one, will this work harm and sorrow to thee."

Seldom is it told of the Buddha that he either smiled or wept. It is said that he smiled for the first time when his father-in-law met him with reproaches at Kapilavastu.

Even the sight of his favourite disciple, Ānanda, in tears by his bedside over his approaching end only draws out the passionless response: "Be of good cheer, Ānanda. Do not weep. Have I not told you oftentimes that this is the regular course of things, that we must part from all that is precious and dear to us? How should it be possible that anything that has arisen should not also pass away?"

And yet the Buddha was human to the core of his being. Once he came upon a sick monk lying helpless and forsaken in his evacuations in his cell. He washed him with his own hands and exhorted his monks thus: "You have neither father nor mother, wherefore be father and mother to one another. As you would tend and wait upon me, so also tend and wait upon the sick". Panthaka, expelled from home, took shelter at the door of the ārāma. "Then came the Lord and stroked my head, and taking me by the arm led me into the garden of the monastery, and out of kindness he gave me a towel for my feet" [*Theragatha*, 557 ff.]. To a woman maddened by grief the congregation said: "Suffer not that little lunatic to come hither." The Exalted One said: "Forbid her not," and, standing near as she came round again, he said to her: "Sister, recover thou presence of mind." She regained her presence of mind "by the sheer potency of the Buddha" [*Psalms of the Sisters*, xlvii.].

He felt an equal concern for the relief of moral suffering. He was intolerent with sin, but not with the sinner. Ajātaśatru, depriving his father of the throne, was not denied his healing words in his remorse. He gave free access to the courtesan, Ambapālī, which made of a lost character an acquisition to society for her liberality. "By the preference designedly given to her over princes and nobles—who, humanly speaking, seemed in every respect better entitled to attentions—one is almost reminded of the conversion of 'a woman that was a sinner' mentioned in the Gospels" [Bishop Bigandet, *Legend of the Buddha*, p. 258]. The Buddha's attitude towards a repentant sinner is thus declared: "Whosoever looks upon his fault as a fault, and rightfully confesses it, shall in the future attain to self-restraint" [*Dīgh. N.* iii. 55).

To monks coming to him from long distances (the monk Soṇa came to him from far off Avantī) he would first address the following words of sympathetic enquiry: "How is it with you, O Monk? Have you lacked for food? Have you had a tiresome journey?"

His humanity and tenderness gave him a sense of humour and a natural humility. Once his favourite pupil Sāriputta burst out: "Such faith have I, Lord, that methinks there never has been nor will be nor is now any other greater or wiser than the Blessed One." "Of course,

Sāriputta,' the Buddha replied, "you have known all the Buddhas of the past." "No, Lord." "Well then, you know those of the future." "No, Lord." "Then at least you know me and have penetrated my mind thoroughly." "Not even that, Lord.' "Then why, Sāriputta, are your words so grand and bold?" [*Mahā. Par. S.* i. 61].

When necessary, he would use the lash of raillery too. Once while the Blessed One sat in meditation under the Vilva tree, there came along the road the distinguished dandy, Daṇḍapāṇi, who, leaning on his walking stick, had the effrontery to ask him: "What does the ascetic profess and preach?" The Buddha's ready wit gave him the suitable answer: "That nothing in the world can put him out of countenance; that perceptions do not adhere to the Holy One, who no longer puts questions, has put an end to all depression, craves neither existence nor non-existence. This I profess, brother: this I preach." Which, in plain English, means: "You don't deserve any attention." "At this reply Daṇḍapāṇi the Śākya drooped his head, and, lolling his tongue, drew his brows up into three wrinkles and went off, hanging on his stick."

Defamation by his enemies could not affect him either. The Lichchhavi chief, Sunakkhatta, "unable to live the holy life under the Buddha," left the Order [*D. N.* iii. 1., 5], and went about Vaiśalī, "proclaiming to all and sundry that the Blessed One has no knowledge of the things that lie beyond the ken of ordinary mortals, that his doctrine is a product of mere reasoning, a thing of his own wit's devising" and so forth [*Maj. N.*]. On Sāriputta reporting this to the Buddha, he calmly said: "Angered, Sāriputta, is this Sunakkhatta, the foolish man. And only of his anger has he said this thing." On another occasion, one of the Bhāradvāja Brāhmans, hearing that their leader had joined the Buddha's Order, "reviled and abused the Exalted One in rude and harsh speeches (saying, 'thou thief, thou fool. . . thou camel . . . thou ass')." The Buddha coolly listened to this vituperation and answered: "Who doth not, when reviled, revile again, a two-fold victory wins." "Abuse that is not answered is like the food rejected by the guest which reverts to th host." Again, a Brāhman householder of Sāvatthī, seeing the Buddha approach him for alms, thus welcomed him: "Stay there, O Shaveling, stay there, O Samaṇaka, stay there, O Vasalaka (outcast)." In both these cases "the scoffers remained to pray" [*Sam. N.* i. 162 and *Vasala Sutta*]. The Buddha was indeed above praise or blame. His standing injunction to his Order was: "Brethren, if outsiders speak against me, the Doctrine, or the Order, or should speak in praise of the same, you should not on the former account bear malice, suffer heart-burning or feel ill-will, nor be filled with pleasure on the latter account" [*Dialogues of the Buddha*, i. 3].

His indifference to praise or blame did not mean any indifference to the truths for which he stood.

His enthusiasm for them and his anxiety to see them spread are thus expressed: "Let a man of intelligence come to me, honest, candid, straightforward; I will instruct him, teach him the Norm, and if he practise according as he is taught, then to know for himself and to realise that supreme religion and goal, for the sake of which clansmen go forth from the household life into the homeless state, will take him—only seven days" [*Di. N.* iii. 56]. This shows the depth of conviction and sincerity which prompted his ministry and made it so compelling and irresistible.

The Buddha's utter humanity may also be illustrated from the relations he had with his monks. An example may be taken from an episode related in the Sutta of the *Holy Goal*:

"Now many monks betook themselves to the venerable Ānanda and said to him: 'It is long, brother Ānanda, since we heard an edifying discourse from the lips of the Exalted One. Good were it, if we might get to hear some.'

" 'Well, venerable ones, betake yourselves to the hermitage of the Brāhman Rammaka. Perhaps you will get to hear an edifying discourse from the lips of the Exalted One.'

" 'That we will do, brother,' replied the monks to the venerable Ānanda."

Then "after the Exalted One had gone from house to house in Sāvatthī and had returned from his begging-round, and finished his meal," he betook himself to the East Grove for the day, and, "when towards evening he had come to the end of his period of meditation," he took his bath and was then led by Ānanda to the hermitage of Rammaka, where many monks assembled were engaged in edifying discourse. "Then the Exalted One stood before the door of the hermitage and awaited the end of their discourse. When now the Exalted One saw that the talk was at an end, he cleared his throat and rapped at the knocker. The monks within opened the door to the Exalted One." Then, entering, he took the seat offered to him and turned to the monks, and so on.

Yet, with all this courtesy and consideration born of his insight into human nature, his characteristic attributes were his passionless detachment, uncompromising idealism, unbending and severe truthfulness, which made him expose the ills of life and prescribe their remedies with a merciless bluntness and rigour without any concession to sentiment, with an elemental simplicity welling up from the depths of his convictions.

The Buddha on principle preferred to take his stand upon the virtues and perfections of human nature and not upon any display of superhuman powers for securing adherents. His feeling on the subject is thus expressed: "It is because I perceive danger in the practice of mystic wonders, that I loathe, and abhor and am ashamed thereof" [*Kevaddha Sutta*]. All kinds of divination, sooth-saying, foretelling or forecasting are condemnend by him as low arts [*Brahma-Jāla Sutta*]. He is equally fair and generous regarding the purposes of his preaching his doctrines. "There are bad things not put away, corrupting, entailing birth renewal, bringing suffering, resulting in ill, making for birth, decay and death in the future. And it is for the putting away of these that I teach the Norm, according to which if ye do walk, the things that corrupt shall be put away, the things that make for purity shall grow and flourish, and ye shall attain to and abide in, each one for himself even here and now, the understanding and the realisation of full and abounding insight—and *not because* I wish to gain pupils, to cause seceding from the rule or mode of living (to which one is wedded by his faith), or to confirm you in bad doctrines or detach you from good doctrines." And thus he has the extraordinary tolerance to say to the follower of a different faith: "Let him who is your teacher be your teacher still. Let that which is your rule be your rule still." With him his truth has to be learnt and lived, and his personality need not be thought of or given any attention at all. He disclaims all ideas of leadership or authority. His rules are the real rulers of his Order.

The Buddha at every step was an example of the precepts and rules he laid down for his monks. "In the days when his reputation stood at its highest point, and his name was named throughout India among the foremost names, one might day by day see that man, before whom kings bowed themselves, walking about, alms-bowl in hand, through streets and alleys, from house to house, and without uttering any request, with downcast look, stand silently waiting until a morsel of food was thrown into his bowl" [Oldenberg]. "At one time," again, as related in a Sutta of the *Aṅguttara Nikāya*, "the Exalted One stayed at Āḷavī, on the cattle-path, in the Siṃsapā forest, upon a couch of leaves, absorbed in meditation in bitterly cold winter, the time of frost," while "rough is the ground troden by the hoofs of the cattle; thin is the couch of leaves; light the monk's yellow robe; sharp the cutting winter wind." When repeatedly asked: "Master, does the Exalted One live happily?" "With sublime uniformity, the Buddha replies: 'It is so, young man. I live happily—of those that live happily in the world I also am one.' "

Or take the following example of his unequalled humility and humanity:

"At that time, at the celebration of Uposatha, on an evening of the full moon, at the annual final assembly of the disciples, before the time of wandering began, the Exalted One sat surrounded by the company of his disciples in the open air.

"Then the Exalted One looked round over the silent company, and said to the monks:

" 'Well, ye disciples, I summon you to say whether you have any fault to find with me, whether in word or in deed' " [*Sam. N.* i. 190].

Again, when a Brāhman asked him, "Does the honoured Gautama permit sleeping in the daytime," he was not ashamed to freely and frankly acknowledge: "In the last month of summer, after the meal, when one has returned from the begging-round, I confess to lying down upon the right side, upon the cloak, folded in four, and, with collected senses, falling asleep." Even his petty foibles are as attractive as his greatness! He is always so careful to disclaim any superhuman attributes: once he says to his disciples, "It is lack of understanding and insight into the Four Holy Truths that is to blame, O Brothers, that we—both you and I—so long have travelled the dreary road of Saṃsāra." We irresistibly feel: "This is the highest; further can no man go!" [Dahlke].

The Buddha also carried his imperturbable dignity into all controversies with his opponents—a proof of both moral and mental power. In the thick of a hard fought intellectual battle he would sit calm, free from any sign of agitation, "his skin of the colour of bright gold," "his countenance all composed," and "his voice like that of a lion roaring." He himself thus declares: "That in disputation with any one whatsoever I could be thrown into confusion or embarrassment,—there is no possibility of such a thing; and, because I know of no such possibility, on that account it is that I remain quiet and confident." And, with an amply justified pride, and self-confidence, he makes the further assertion in frankness to his favourite disciple, Sāriputta: "And, when ye shall carry me hither upon a bed, the intellectual vigour of the Perfect One will remain unabated." The pilgrim, Pilotika, gives a fine testimony to this 'intellectual vigour' by describing how he has seen learned Kṣatriyas, Brāhmans, and ascetics, all accomplished controversialists, cleaving through fabrics of views or systems of thought by their hair-splitting wit, coming to the Buddha with a plan to trap him and trip him with cunningly devised questions, only to be convinced, confounded and converted by his discourse [*Maj. N.* i. 175 *sqq*.]. His success and calmness in debate were also very well shown when he was challenged to a disputation by the naked ascetic, Sachchaka, in the presence of 500 Lichchhavi chiefs at Vaiśālī. Sachchaka took up the position that the Body is one's Self, which the Buddha refutes thus : If the body is one's self, can any one control his body in the same way in which, for example, kings like Pasenadi and Ajātasattu, or the republics of the Vajjis and Mallas can control their own domains, in which they exercise powers of life and death, outlawry and banishment? In the end Sachchaka confessed : "Verily, honoured Gautama, we have been perverse and presumptuous in thinking that in argument we might triumph over you. A man might as well go up to an impassioned elephant, to a blazing mass of fire or to a poisonous reptile, unscathed. Will the honoured Gotama with his disciples deign to accept food from me to-morrow?"

And, lastly, what further makes him great is that he made his spirituality consistent with the positivist ideal of social service. He was in the world and yet not of it. In the sphere of Politics and Statecraft his advice was eagerly sought. Princes vied with peasants to honour and follow him. If there is a feud between the Śākyas and the Koliyas which may end in bloodshed, it is the arbitration of an ascetic that is invoked and stops it! If the Emperor of Magadha has a plan to crush the liberties of a neighbouring republic, the Buddha's opinion is to be first sought on its prospects! If there is a new chief appointed for the Śākya state, the Buddha must first address him a discourse! Even the crimes of emperors were confessed to him with promise of amendment! He showed interest too in the wars of his times, *e.g.* the two wars between Pasenadi, then king of both Kosala and Kāśī, and Ajātaśatru, in the first of which the former had to retreat and in the second captured the latter, "his nephew," alive [*Sam. N.* i. 81-83]; also the war between Viḍūḍabha of Kosala and the Śākyas, which he vainly tried to prevent. Pasenadi, the follower of the Buddha from his youth upwards, consulted him on every point, whether it was a meal, the birth of a daughter, daily habits, the death of a grandmother at 120, law and judgment, or a war [*ibid*]. Thus, by instructing kings, the Buddha could influence their administration and the well-being of their peoples. The monarchies and free states of the period, mutually hostile, like the Śākyas and Kosala, or the Lichchhavis and Magadha, were at one in seeking and honouring him. He had a free passage and warm welcome everywhere.

Great in life, the Buddha was greater even in death. The founder of a system found no place for himself in it in life or after death. The original Buddhism is independent of the Buddha himself, who in his personal aspect does not count at all. No other religion in the world can show such self-effacement in its founder! When nearing his end, he was approached by Ānanda for instructions touching the Order, and received a reply bringing out his characteristic greatness: "What, then, Ānanda? Does the Order expect that of me? I have preached the truth without making any distinction between exoteric and esoteric doctrine, for the Tathāgata has no such thing as the closed fist of a teacher, who keeps some things back...Now the Tathāgata thinks not that it is he who should lead the brotherhood, or that the Order is dependent upon him. Why then should he leave instructions in any matter concerning the Order?

"Therefore, O Ānanda, be ye lamps unto yourselves. Be ye a refuge to yourselves. Betake yourselves to no external refuge. Hold fast to the truth as a lamp. Hold fast as a refuge to the truth. Look not for refuge to any one besides yourselves."

In the same spirit he says that "the brother or the sister who continually fulfils all the greater and lesser duties, who is correct in life, observing the precepts—it is he who rightly honours him with the worthiest homage". And, lastly, when Ānanda still asks him: "What are we to do,

Lord, with the remains of the Tathāgata ?" his final admonishing answer is: "Hinder not yourselves, Ānanda, by honouring the remains of the Tathāgata. Be zealous, I beseech you, Ānanda, in your behalf! Devote yourselves to your own good! Be earnest, be zealous, be intent on your own good!

"And after I am gone, let the Truths and Rules of the Order which I have set forth and laid down for you all, be the Teacher to you!"

We may sum up the features of his career and character in the admirable words put into the mouth of the Soṇadaṇḍa, the learned Brāhman of Champā, to an assembly of 500 Brāhmans sojourning in that city:

"Truly, Sirs, the venerable Gotama is well born on both sides, of pure descent through the father and mother back through seven generations, with no slur put upon them, and no reproach in respect of birth.

"He has gone forth into the religious life, giving up the great clan of his relations, much money and gold, and treasure;

"While he was still a young man, without a grey hair on his head, in the beauty of his early manhood;

"Though his father and mother were unwilling, and wept, their cheeks being wet with tears, he nevertheless cut off his hair and beard, and donned the yellow robes, and went out from the household life into the homeless state.

"He is handsome, pleasant to look upon, inspiring trust, gifted with great beauty of complexion, fair in colour, fine in presence, stately to behold;

"He is virtuous with the virtue of the Arahats, good and virtuous;

"He has a pleasant voice and a pleasing delivery, gifted with polite address, distinct, not husky, suitable for making clear the matter in hand.

"He is the teacher of the teachers of many, one who puts righteousness in the forefront of his exhortations to the Brāhman race.

"Of him people come right across the country from distant lands to ask questions, and he bids all men welcome, is congenial, conciliatory, not supercilious, accessible to all, not backward in conversation.

"Whereas some Samaṇas and Brāhamans have gained a reputation by all sorts of insignificant matters ('such as by wearing no clothes,' etc.), his reputation comes from perfection in conduct and righteousness.

"And he is trusted, honoured and venerated by the King of Magadha, Seniya Bimbisāra, King Pasenadi of Kosala and even by the leading Brāhman teacher Pokkharasādi with their children and wives, their people and courtiers or intimates" [*Soṇadaṇḍa Sutta*].

Of the Buddha it could not be said that "the prophet is not honoured in his own home." The contemporary popularity and reverence commanded by him gained him a warm reception and hospitality everywhere, and among all classes and ranks of society. Among his hosts figure emperors like Bimbisāra [*Mahā. V.* i. 22], ministers of state like Sunīdha and Vassakāra [*Mahā. Par. Sutta*, i. 30], merchant princes like the Seṭṭhi of Rājagṛiha and Anāthapiṇḍika [*Chulla Vagga*, vi. 4. 1], leaders of orthodox sects like the Brāhman Kassapa [*M. V.* i. 16], military leaders like Sīha, the commander-in-chief of the Lichchhavis [*ib.* vi. 25], aristocratic ladies like Ambapālī of Vaiśālī [*M. Par. S.* ii], Suppiyā of Benares [*M. V.*], of Viśākhā, who gave garments to monks, besides ordinary poorer folks and householders of different castes, like Chunda the smith [*ib.* 36]. Nor were the peoples of republics less eager to honour and entertain him than the peoples under monarchies. The Mallas of Kusinārā "established a compact to the effect that whosoever went not forth to welcome the Blessed One should pay a fine of 500 pieces." The citizens of Kusinārā also agreed among themselves to provide food for the Order by turns definitely fixed. But perhaps a record in hospitality was that of Meṇḍaka the householder, who, after daily entertaining the Order during their sojourn in his city of Bhaddiyanagara in the Magadha kingdom, followed them in their travels with cartloads of supplies, salt, oil, rice and hard food, and with 1250 cow-keepers in charge of as many cows for the supply of fresh milk to as many Bhikṣus! Even non-Buddhists figure as some of his most enthusiastic hosts—a compliment to the Buddha's humanity, which, standing above caste and creed, commanded universal recognition. Such was Keṇiya the Jaṭila of Āpaṇa [*Sutta Nipata*, iii. 7, 21-22], who gave the Buddha and his 250 disciples a sumptuous dinner followed by a discourse by the Buddha touching some essential points in Brāhmanism. Another was "a certain high official at court" of Magadha, who was a follower of the Ājīvikas [*Chulla V*. vi. 10, 1.]. Sometimes we read of the Buddha sitting by the sacred fire of a Brāhaman and discoursing, but not denouncing his worship [*Maj. N*. 75].

Indeed the Buddha did not take any advantage of the goodness of his hosts, or abuse their hospitality in any way. He was very particular and scrupulous to ensure that no person giving him an opportunity for discourse after dinner changed his own faith and sect in a hurry under his temporary influence. Thus he asked Uruvelā Kassapa, the leader of 500 Jaṭila followers, "to go first and inform them of his intentions" to desert them and join the Buddhist Order, and was careful to withdraw his presence from Kassapa, lest it should affect his reputation which drew to him "all the people of Aṅga and Magadha" with presents of "abundant food, both hard and soft" [*M. V*. i. 18, 20]. In accepting the Commandant Sīha as his disciple, he strongly exhorted him not to withdraw his support from his quondam co-religionists, lest they should be left helpless [*M. V*. vi. 31, 11]. Indeed it is stated that in preaching he showed more zeal for his own monks, then for lay-believers, and then the Brāhmans.

ascetics, and followers of other sects, "like the landowner sowing the good field, the middling field, and last the bad one" [*Sam. N.* xlii. 7].

The Indian view of the Buddha's life and work is best given by that profound Western student of Buddhism, Paul Dahlke:

"Perhaps never while the world has lasted has there been a personality who has wielded such a tremendous influence over the thinking of humanity as has Gautama, the bearer of the Buddha-thought. This statement becomes indubitable fact for every one who rids himself of the baseless obscurantism which by the word 'world' understands only the centre of Greco-Roman Christian culture, and the radiations in time and space that proceed from that centre. Again, this statement becomes an undeniable fact for every one who has learnt to understand by culture something else besides the mere art of living comfortably and making money quickly;—who has learnt to understand that progress does not proceed upon outward lines, but that true development consists of that inwardness which seeks and tries to comprehend that of which either the world knows nothing or which it treats with indifference, perhaps even with contempt. Whoso recognises this will also recognise that already, almost two and a half milleniums ago, the supreme summit of spiritual development was reached, and that at that distant time, in the quiet hermit groves along the Ganges, already had been thought the highest man can think. He will recognise that with time it is only the shell that has changed, never the kernel, the manner of expression, never the thing expressed, and that in the endless milleniums yet to come it will never be otherwise. For higher thought there is not than that Buddha-thought which wipes out the world, and with it its bearer.

"These were those times in the which a life devoted to the search for the highest, for a felicity beyond all that the world could give was not considered madness, but as something worthy of all honour. These were the times, the unique times, in which it seemed natural not only to preach the good and the true, but also to live it. If such consistent uniformity can be ascribed to any men at all, then most surely is Gautama the Buddha among such men." (*Buddhist Essays*, pp. 18-9.)

ASOKA

(274-236 B.C.)

It has been very often and widely assumed that while the ancient Hindus had a genius for abstract speculation, producing so many systems of philosophy and religion, they were notoriously deficient in all practical skill and capacities, so that the spiritual interests of life were disproportionately cultivated to the neglect of its material interests. The reign of Asoka, and, indeed, the entire history of India, is a refutation of this assumption. Students of Indian history in all its aspects, political, economic, and cultural, cannot but realise and recognise that India was great not merely in her literature, her philosophy, her religion, and her spirituality, but also in her arts and crafts, which built up her material prosperity and gave her a commanding position for her many manufactures and precious products among the trading nations of the world. Under Asoka India reached the high-water mark of this material progress, and, in a sense, of moral progress too. She demonstrated her greatness as much in the sphere of ideals as in the sphere of practical achievements.

Coming by inheritance into the possession of a vast empire that extended from Afghanistan to Mysore, Asoka proceeded to endow and adorn it with manifold works of art and utility: with cities and palaces, stūpas and cave-dwellings in rocks, ornamental architecture and sculpture, showing finely executed figures of animals, birds, plants and flowers; with reservoirs, dams and sluices for irrigation; with wells, roads lined with trees and rest-houses for travellers; hospitals for both men and animals, and botanical gardens for the culture of medicinal plants as sources of medicines for the people, and so forth. Together with this elaborate apparatus for the physical necessities, comforts and enjoyments of life, Asoka gave to his empire certain principles of administration which, in their breadth of vision and outlook, their spirit of humanity and internationalism, are an aspiration even to the modern world. He based his empire upon the principle of Ahiṃsā, of Non-Violence, Universal Peace, Peace between Man and Man, and between Man and every sentient creature, so that it was an empire of Righteousness, an empire resting on Right and not on Might, and thus too far ahead of the times to stand the ordained and ordinary historic process of a painful development from the brute to the man! He also gave to his subject peoples of different communities, castes, and creeds, certain common and cardinal ideals of thought and conduct which make him to be humanity's first teacher of Universal Morality-

and Religion. These principles of Policy and Morality may be read to this day on the rocks and proclamation pillars on which they were inscribed in imperishable characters in the different provinces of his far-flung empire. These 'sermons in stone' are a sort of autobiography of the emperor, and the most important and fruitful sources of his remarkable history.

Firstly, let us trace the history and success of his practical achievements, as written in his material monuments, before we study his moral achievements, his contributions in the sphere of ideals. The most interesting of these monuments are his inscriptions, of which the idea, being new to Indian history, is supposed to have been suggested to Asoka by a foreign precedent, the inscriptions of the Persian emperor Darius. The inscriptions, meant to be read by the people at large, were necessarily located at all important centres of population in the country, and, as they were meant to last for a long time, they were engraved on the most durable material, stone. Thus the double need of publicity and permanence practically determined the geographical distribution of the edicts of Asoka. Where Nature failed to supply the facilities for the publication of the edicts, the aid of Art was invoked: huge monolithic columns were specially fashioned for the purpose and planted in places where a suitable rocky surface was not available to receive the emperor's message in inscriptions. One of the edicts itself informs us that "this message of the emperor must be written on the rocks or wherever there are blocks or pillars of stone (*silāṭhubhe silāṭhaṃbhasi*)" [Minor Rock Edict I., Rūpnāth text]. Thus the edicts are of two classes, the Rock Edicts and the Pillar Edicts.

The Rock Edicts, numbering fourteen in one corpus, are found at thirteen different localities within an area embracing as many as twenty degrees of latitude and thirteen of longitude. These localities are:

(1) Shāhbāzgarhī, near Peshawar, in the North-Western Frontier Province, where the edicts are inscribed on a mass of trap rock, 24 feet long and 10 feet high, on the slope of a hill. A separate rock close by bears the twelfth edict, emphasising the principle of toleration among a people who probably specially needed it.

(2) Mānsērā, also in the North-Western Frontier Province, where the Toleration Edict appears by itself on one side of the rock.

Both these edicts are given a further local colouring by being inscribed in the current scripts of the localities concerned, the Kharoṣṭhī written from right to left.

(3) Kālsī near Dehra Dun, where the record is incised on a white quartz boulder at the confluence of the Jumna and Tons rivers, which must have been a populous centre.

(4) Sopārā in the Thānā district of Bombay Presidency, famous as the port of Sūrpāraka in old Pāli texts, on the sea-coast.

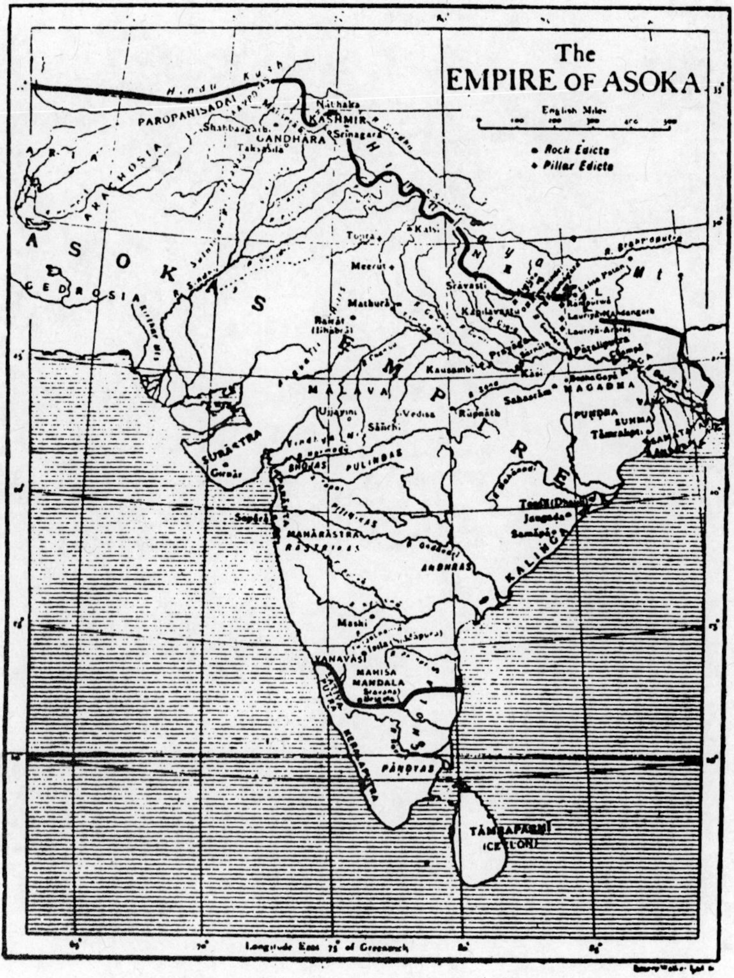
The
EMPIRE OF ASOKA
English Miles
100
200
300
400
500
Rock Edicts
Pillar Edicts
Hindu Kush
PAROPANISADAI
Nathaka
KASHMIR
Srinagara
Shahbazgarhi
GANDHARA
Taksasila
ARACHOSIA
ASOKA'S
GEDROSIA
EMPIRE
Topra
Kalsi
Meerut
Sravasti
Mathura
Kapilavastu
Bairat
Prayaga
Pataliputra
Kausambi
Kasi
MALAVA
Sahasram
MAGADHA
Ujjayini
Vedisa
Rupnath
Sanchi
PUNDRA
SUMHA
Tamralipti
SURASTRA
Girnar
BHOJAS
PULINDAS
Sopara
MAHARASTRA
RASTRIKAS
Tosali (Dhauli)
Jaugada
Samapa
KALINGA
ANDHRAS
Maski
VANAVASI
MAHISA
MANDALA
PANDYAS
TAMBAPANNI
(CEYLON)
Longitude East 75° of Greenwich

(5) Girnār in Kathiwar, where the edicts are inscirbed on a granite rock on the margin of the lake or reservoir constructed for purposes of irrigation by Chandragupta Maurya and completed under Asoka, with the sluices and supplemental channels to be described later.

(6) Dhaulī in the Purī district of Orissa, where the inscription is made on a sloping sheet of stone specially prepared for the purpose. The place is called Tosalī in the Kaliṅga Edict appearing there.

(7) Jaugaḍa in the Ganjām district, where the inscription is on a rock of granitic gneiss at the centre of the old town, then probably known as Samāpā (of the Kaliṅga Rock Edict I.).

These two versions of the edicts in the province of Kaliṅga newly conquered by Asoka omit Edicts XI., XII. and XIII., as being locally unsuitable, and introduce in their place some new and more appropriate, ones, which may be designated as the Borderers' and Provincials' Edicts, or the Kaliṅga Edicts I. and II.

(8) Chitaldurg in Mysore, where in three different localities, viz. Siddāpura (probably Isila of the inscription), Jatinga-Rāmeśvara and Brahmagiri, occur what are called the Minor Rock Edicts I. and II., the earliest of the Asokan Edicts. These Mysore Edicts seem to have been issued from the office of the Prince and Viceroy of Suvarṇagiri in the Deccan.

(9) Rūpnāth in the Jubbulpur district, where the Minor Rock Edict I. was inscribed on a detached boulder near three pools, one above

another, by a Śiva temple on a rock, still the attraction of pilgrims.

(10) Sahasrām in the Shāhābād district of Behār, where the Minor Rock Edict I. is inscribed on a rocky surface within an artificial cave near the summit of a hill.

(11) Bairāt in Rājpūtāna, where the Minor Rock Edict I. is engraved on a block of volcanic rocks, as big as a house, close to the ancient town of that name.

(12) Maskī in the Nizam's dominions, where also appears the Minor Rock Edict I.

It may be noted that a special importance attaches to the Minor Rock Edict I., published as it was in so many widely separated localities.

(13) Bhābrā in Rājpūtāna, where the boulder was brought from Bairāt, on which was inscribed a special edict citing some passages of Buddhist scripture together with the Minor Rock Edict I. The two inscriptions were incised on the boulder within the precincts of a Buddhist monastery on the top of a second hill at Bairāt.

It will thus appear that, true to the directions contained in Minor Rock Edict I., the inscriptions were imprinted on rocky surfaces (*Parvatesu*) near a river, as in Kālsī, or a lake, as at Girnār, or on detached boulders (*śilāstūpa*), as in most other places.

The '*śilāstambhas*,' or Pillars of Stone, bearing the other edicts of the emperor, were found at the following places: (1) Toprā in Ambālā district; (2) Meerut; (3) Kauśāmbī, on which are inscribed

Pillar Edicts I.-VI., the Queen's Edict, and what is called the Kauśāmbī Edict; (4) Lauriyā-Ararāj in the Champāran district; (5) Lauriyā-Nandangarh in the same district; (6) Rāmpūrwā in the same district; (7) Sāñchī near Bhopāl, bearing the Minor Pillar, Sārnāth Pillar and Kauśāmbī Pillar Edicts in variants ; (8) Sārnāth near Benares ;. (:) Rummindei in Nepal ; (10) Niglīvā in the Nepalese Tarai.

These Asokan Pillars are a triumph of engineering, architecture and sculpture. Huge and entire monoliths were extracted, handled and chiselled to be shaped into these pillars weighing about 50 tons and about as high as 50 feet. The blocks of stone seem to have been all quarried in the hills of Chunar, the only source in the neighbourhood of the fine sandstone of which the pillars are uniformly composed. It was thus a problem in transport to carry so many gigantic shafts from the place of their manufacture to their distant destinations. The difficulty of the problem might be realised from the fact that many centuries later, in A.D. 1356, Sultan Firoz Shah had the Toprā pillar removed to Delhi, a short distance, by employing as many as 8400 men to draw the cart on which it was placed, 200 men pulling at each of its 42 wheels! But the pillars, though huge in height and weight, showed the most delicate and artistic workmanship. Firstly, they showed a polish "which no modern mason knows how to impart to the material," as admitted by Vincent Smith.

Secondly, they are furnished with beautifully designed and executed capitals, comprising (1) a bell-shaped part of the Persepolitan pattern, which is however supposed by Havell to be a lotus; (2) an abacus above it, circular or oblong, which serves as a pedestal for (3) an animal, like a lion, as on the pillars at Lauriyā-Nandangarh and Rāmpūrwā, the uninscribed pillar at Bakhira in Muzaffarpur district, or a bull, as on the uninscribed pillar at Rāmpūrwā, or an elephant, or a Garuḍa as at Lauriyā-Ararāj. Sometimes, instead of a single lion, there are four lions placed back to back, as on the pillars at Sāñchī and Sārnāth, with a stone wheel, the 'wheel of darma,' between them. Sir John Marshall considers both bell and lions as masterpieces in point of both style and technique. The abacus on the Lauriyā-Nandangarh Pillar is further decorated on the margin with a bas-relief representing a row of geese pecking their food (probably symbolical of the flock of the Buddha's disciples), while that on the Allahābād-Kauśāmbī Pillar a scroll of "altrenate lotus and honeysuckle resting on a beaded astragalus moulding."

In the case of one pillar, the ūniscribed one at Rāmpūrwā, it has been found that the bell-shaped part was joined on to the shaft by a bolt of pure copper of the form of a barrel with a length of 2 feet $\frac{1}{2}$ inch, diameter of $4\frac{5}{16}$ inches in the centre and $3\frac{5}{8}$ inches at each end.

Asoka is also credited in tradition with the construction of as many as 84,000 stūpas (for

84,000 atoms of the bones of the Buddha's body, or, according to another version, for the 84,000 sections of the Dharma), of which Yuan Chwang came to know of 80, and only two have been up to now unearthed, those at Sāñchī and Bharhut. The Niglīvā Pillar inscription informs us that Asoka had twice enlarged the stūpa of Buddha Koṇāgamana.

Commodious chambers with interiors shining like mirrors were also excavated in the most refractory rock, the hard gneiss of the Barabar Hills, as the emperor's gifts to the sect of the Ājīvikas.

Asoka was also the builder of cities and palaces. He is said to have founded Śrīnagar, the capital of Kashmir, where he built 500 monasteries, of which 100 were seen by Yuan Chwang. In Nepal he built the city of Deo-pātan, called after his son-in-law Devapāla, who with his daughter Chārumatī chose to settle there. At the capital of the Mauryan empire, Pāṭaliputra, Asoka made many improvements in replacing the old wooden material of the palace by stone, and by executing elegant carving and inlaid sculpture-work "which no human hands of this world could accomplish," as observed by Fa-hien.

Asoka also brought to a completion the magnificent irrigation work commenced by Chandragupta Maurya. It was a reservoir or lake, called Sudarśana, constructed on Mount Ūrjayat by artificially damming up the flow of several streams of that mount, the Suvarṇasikatā,

Palāśinī and others, as described in a later inscription (of Rudradāman, 150 A.D.). It is also stated in the same inscription that the lake was of "a structure so well joined as to rival the spur of a mountain." It was "ordered to be made by the Vaiśya Puṣyagupta, the provincial governor (*rāṣṭriya*) of the Maurya king, Chandragupta, adorned with conduits for Asoka the Maurya by the Yavana king, Tuṣāspha, while governing (*adhiṣṭhāya*)." Thus the reservoir was equipped "with well-provided conduits, drains and means to guard against foul matter," as stated in the inscription. In connexion with these irrigation works of the Mauryan emperors we may note that Megasthenes also has referred to Mauryan officers, whose duty was "to measure the land, and inspect the *sluices* by which water is distributed into the branch canals, so that every one may enjoy his fair share of the benefit."

Lastly, we may also refer to his other works of public utility inspired by non-economic, humanitarian considerations. These may be best described in his own words [P.E. VII.]: "On the roads I have had banyan trees planted to give shade to man and beast; I have had groves of mango-trees planted; at every half-kos I have had wells dug; rest-houses have been erected; and numerous watering-places have been provided by me here and there for the enjoyment of man and beast." In another edict [R.E. II.] he refers to his work in providing, in hospitals, for medical aid and treatment for both men and beasts, and, in botanical gardens and pharmaceutical works, for the supply of medicines from the approved medicinal herbs, roots and fruits, obtained by import where necessary.

We shall now consider the paractical achievements of Asoka in a different sphere, the sphere of administration. The art of government, of imperial administration, is by no means less practical than the other arts of civilised life like engineering or architecture. It calls for practical ability, insight into the needs and conditions of men, and capacity for business and organisation not so necessary for the technical and mechanical expert.

Nor was the problem of government an easy one for the Mauryan emperors. The area of government was too wide to be conveniently controlled from one centre by a single authority. The area is apparent from the very distribution of Asoka's inscriptions, proclaiming his authority and message from the northern frontiers to Mysore associated with the sacred memory of his grandfather's retirement in religious life. The area was further extended by Asoka's conquest of Kalinga, signalized by 150,000 persons carried away as captives, 100,000 wounded and many times that number succumbing to their wounds or other after-effects of war. There was also much suffering caused indirectly to the civilian population of the country related to the combatants affected in the war by blood or by other ties of friendship or dependence. This almost modern appraisement of the violence wrought by his first war made Asoka determine that it should be his last and attached him earnestly to a more humane creed of Non-Violence, viz. Buddhism. Thus his empire ceased to extend at the expense of the freedom of the neighbouring states and peoples, which was henceforth to be scrupulously respected. Thus we find that the Mauryan empire at the height of its power and glory did not include all parts and peoples of India.

But it was sufficiently extensive to call for the highest administrative skill and statesmanship in devising a suitable form of government for the different regions committed to its care. A large part of this work was done under the first Mauryan emperor. But it was felt to Asoka to introduce some important innovations, which are indicated in the edicts.

The government had necessarily to be multi-central. A unitary, centralised administration could not hope to control an empire larger than British India in those pre-mechanical ages of primitive transport. Thus the empire was split up into a number of provincial administrations and viceroyalties modelled on a common plan. The head of the government was, of course, the sovereign, whose authority was in theory, or in the legal sense, unlimited. But in practice it was limited in many ways under the established usages and cutoms of the Hindu state. The Hindu King could not be an absolute despot like the Czar or the Sultan. He was not the source

CAPITAL OF ASOKAN PILLAR AT SARNATH

as restored in its original form (based on Plate *V*, Fig. 1 of Percy Brown's *Indian Architecture*) which places the *Dharma-chakra* (Wheel of Religion) on the shoulders of the Four Lions set back to back (as on view at the Sarnath Museum at Banaras). The original wheel was severed from the Pillar and broken into fragments kept in the Museum. The symbolism of this device is the supremacy of the spiritual (represented in the *Dharma-chakra*) over the physical or brute force (as represented in the lions).

and fountain of all law in the country. Part of it was sacred law governing social life, whose sources were independent of the sovereign, viz. (*a*) the Vedas; (*b*) the Smṛitis; (*c*) the practices of the pious (*śiṣṭāchāra*); and (*d*) the opinions of the pious on doubtful points, while much of the ordinary secular law had its origin in the many groups and communities in the country which legislated for themselves. There was no central sovereign or legislature that legislated for the entire country. The laws of the realm were not uniform or standardised, but were various according to various local conditions. Thus castes, country people (*jānapada*), guilds and families were permitted to make their own laws, which were respected by the sovereign or the state. Along with the legislative functions, the executive and judicial functions of the sovereign were also considerably decentralised. The result was that the people were practically self-governing in the various groups and communities to which they belonged. The Hindu state, like some of the more advanced of modern democracies in the West, encouraged group-life and the vital and natural associations, and was thus autocratic only in name or theory. Its autocracy was limited from below by a vast subterranean democracy, a self-governing society moving in its own orbit, apart from the state.

Asoka emphasised still further the moral foundations of his authority, his responsiblity to his people as the guardian of their well-being.

He was fond of declaring that all men were his children, for whom as their father he desired every kind of prosperity and happiness both in this world and the next [K.E. I.] and that his governors were created for the welfare and happiness of the governed, who were committed to their care as a child is committed to a skilful nurse [P.E. IV.]. And his sense of responsibility to his people made him work very hard as a public servant. In Rock Edict VI. he comments on the lapses of his predecessors, and makes a public declaration that he will be ready for public business at all hours and places even while at meals or in his bedroom or in his meditations. Even while thus working, he never "felt satisfied with his exertions and despatch of business" [*ib.*]. And the spirit which sustained him in his work was that thereby he was only "obtaining his own release from the debt he owed to his fellow human beings" [*ib.*].

The sovereign's main work in the administration was naturally that of supervision, for which he depended upon a special class of officers called the *Prativedakas* [R.E. VI.], who would report to him on public affairs at all hours. He was also assisted by a Pariṣad of Ministers, *Mahāmātrus* [R.E. III. and VI.], or the Privy Council, whose number, according to Kauṭilya, depended upon the needs of administration. But he depended upon himself mostly for his own work. That the master's eye might be everywhere in his dominions, he initiated the practice of travelling through them, not in search of pleasure or sport like his predecessors, but for "the inspection of the country and the people" (*jañapadasya janasya darśanam*, R.E. VIII.). But so "great was his dominion" that he could not visit all its principal parts marked out by his edicts, for he assumes, and apologises for, mistakes in their writing when there are practially none [R.E. XIV.]. Besides receiving reports and travelling, the emperor's work comprised the issue of notifications or edicts, in which the following matters are dealt with, in a broad sense: (1) The policy of his government [in R.E. XIII, K.E. I. and II. and R.E. IV.]; (2) the special laws passed by him for protection of life [R.E. I., P.E. V.] and reprieve of three days granted to convicts sentenced to death [P.E. IV.]; (3) the powers and duties of his governors and his injunctions to them [P.E. IV., K.E. II.]; (4) his orders regarding periodical tours of all his officers; (5) his institution of a new Department of Morals and the duties of its staff R.E. V.]; (6) the sovereign's own duties and example [M.R.E. I., R.E. I., R.E. VI., R.E. VIII., P.E. II.]; (7) the moral ideals prescribed for his people [M.R.E. II., R.E. IV., VII., IX., X., XI., XII., P.E. I., III., VI.]; (8) his public works of utility and other innovations [R.E. II., P.E. VII.]. It is apparent that all these subjects should fall within the province of the emperor's personal administration.

Next to the emperor ranked the viceroys in charge of the larger provinces. The viceroys were generally recruited from the princes of the blood royal, called Kumāras and Āryaputras in the edicts, which mention four such viceroys, viz. those at Taxilā, Ujjain, Tosalī and Suvarṇagiri. According to tradition Asoka, as prince, was viceroy at Taxilā. He himself is said to have appointed Prince Kuṇāla as his viceroy there. According to Fa-hien [Lagge's tr., p. 31] he appointed his son, Prince Dharma-Vivardhana, as his viceroy of Gandhāra. Like the king, the viceroys had also their ministers [cf. M.R.E. I., K.R.E.].

The smaller provinces were under officers called Rāṣṭriyas [Rudradāman's inscription cited above] and Rājūkas. The governor of the western province under Chandragupta was Puṣyagupta, the Vaiśya, and under Asoka, Rājā Tuṣāpha, the Yavana. The Rājūkas are spoken of as being "set over hundreds of thousands of souls" [R.E. III., P.E. IV.]. They were not created by Asoka, but were invested by him with larger powers as regards award of honours and penalties. There were other provincial officers, called the Prādeśikas [R.E. III.], in charge of the executive, revenue and judicial service [see *JRAS*, 1914, pp. 383-6], while the Rājūkas, as suggested by the name itself [—rajjugrāhakas, *i.e.* land-measurers], would deal with "survey, land settlement and irrigation" [see *Cambridge History*, pp. 487, 508]. There were also other officers of a similar rank, called the Puruṣas, spoken of as being "set over the multitude" [P.E. VII.], whose duty was to exhort the Rājūkas into loyal service of the king [P.E. IV.]. Bühler considers them to be like the Prativedakas or the inspectorate of the government.

The Heads of Departments are sometimes called Mukhas [P.E. VII.]. They were also called the Mahāmātras. The department assigned to a Mahāmātra was indicated by its name being prefixed to that of the officer. Thus the Dharma-Mahāmātras were in charge of the department of Dharma, the Strī-adhyakṣa-mahāmātras in charge of superintendents of women, the Anta-Mahāmātras of the frontiers [P.E. I.]. The Mahāmātras, who were the Prefects of cities, were called the *Nagara-vyāvahārikas*[1] [K.E.], such as those at Tosalī (which was under a viceroy), Isila and Samāpā. *Dūtas* or envoys are also mentioned, but they seem to have belonged to the class of

[1]Of the two Kaliṅga Edicts, one is addressed to the Mahāmātras who were *Nagaravyāvahārikas* and the other in the Jaugaḍa version is addressed to Mahāmātras described as *Lajavachanikas*, *i.e.* those to whom the king could address directly his messages. The latter class of Mahāmātras would be like the provincial governors, and there was no princely viceroy between them and the king. Thus Samāpā was *not* under a prince, while Tosalī *was*. The second Kaliṅga Edict is addressed in the Dhaulī version to the Kumāra *as well as* the Mahāmātras, probably the ministers of the viceroy. Thus it may be assumed that while Tosalī, *i.e.* Dhaulī, was the seat of a viceroyalty, Samāpā, *i.e.* Jaugada, was the seat of a governorship. Tosalī, it may be noted, figures as the capital of Kaliṅga under Khāravela in his famous Hāthigumphā cave inscription.

officers called Dharma-Mahāmātras [R.E. XIII.]. The ordinary civil servants were called *Yuktas* [R.E. III.] and *Puruṣas*, distinguished as being of high, low, or middle rank [P.E. I.]. The clerk, scribe, *lipikara*, is also mentioned [M.R.E. II., Brahmagiri text].

The most inportant administrative innovation of Asoka was his creation of a new department for the spread of the Dharma as defined by him, and his recognition of the principle that the first care of the state was the moral development of the people. The edicts adumbrate the growth of this idea in Asoka's mind. In the Kaliṅga Rock Edict II. he first expresses his feeling that all might not be well with the administration, and calls upon his officers to see that no man is put under imprisonment or torture without due cause. And "for this purpose, in accordance with Dharma," to prevent all injustice, he declared his resolve that he "shall send forth in rotation every five years such persons as are of mild and temperate disposition, and regardful of the sanctity of life, who, knowing this purpose, will comply with his instructions." A similar order was sent out to the princely viceroys of Ujjain and Taxilā that they should at least every three years send on tour similar bodies of officials for the same purpose. Later this intention of the emperor was developed into a standing decree, announced in his Rock Edict III., by which it was ordained that "everywhere in his dominions his officers of all ranks—the Yuktas, the Rājūkas and the Prādeśikas—

must go out on tours (*anusaṃyāna*), each every five years, as well for their ordinary administrative business as for this special purpose, the inculcation of the Dharma." Next, after a year, this scheme of religious tours by his officials received a further development in the institution of a special class of officers, the Dharma-Mahāmātras, charged with the duty of attending to the moral and spiritual welfare of all his subjects, irrespective of their creed or community, Brāhmans, Buddhists, Jains, Ājvīkas and others [P.E. VII.], or "soldiers and their chiefs, the rich and the destitute, the old and the infirm," or members of the royal family, male and female, both in the capital and provincial towns [R.E. V.].

Their first duty was to prevent and remedy unjust molestation, imprisonment and execution (*paribādha*, *bandhana* and *vadha*). Their more general duty was to spread and establish the Dhamra (*dharmādhiṣṭhāna*) and regulate the charities (*anugrahika* of P.E. VII) both of the king, and of the queens (*dānaviṣaya*, *ib.*) and the princes (*ib.*); for the Dharma was connected with charities. Theirs was also the delicate task of supervising female morals, and in that capacity they were called Strī-adhyakṣa-mahāmātras [R.E. XII.]. They also seem to have been in charge of the various kinds of works of public utility in the country, such as provision of hospitals, medical aid, medicines, drinking water and rest-houses for travellers and the like, as will be apparent from Rock Edict II. and Rock Edict

XIII., if they are read together. Lastly, their work was also to organise the foreign missions which are so unique a feature of Asoka's administration. The missions were at work both "in the dominions of His Majesty (and also among his frontagers (*pratyantesu*)" [R.E. II.]. Among these 'frontagers' are mentioned the Yavanas, Kāmbojas, Gandhāras in the north-west, Rāṣṭrikas, Pitinikas [R.E. V.], Nābhapantis, Bhojas, Andhras and Pulindas in the interior, and the Cholas and Pāṇḍayas, the Satiyaputra and Keralaputra in the south [R.E. II., V. and XIII.]. Dūtas or envoys were also sent on missionary work among distant foreign states beyond the 'frontagers,' viz. Egypt under Ptolemy Philadelphos (285-47 B.C.), Macedonia under Antigonos Gonatas (278-39 B.C.), Cyrene under Magas (285-58 B.C.), Epirus under an Alexander (272-? 258 B.C.) and Syria under Antiochos Theos (261-46 B.C.), all mentioned in Rock Edict XIII., and also referred to in Rock Edict II.

On the subject of these foreign missions of Asoka, some reliable information is given in the literary source, *Mahāvaṃsa* [v. 280], which relates that at the conclusion of the proceedings of the third Buddhist Council held at Pāṭaliputra in the nineteenth year of Asoka's coronation, the President, Moggaliputta Tissa (called Upagupta in the northern texts) "sent forth theras, one here and one there," for evangelising work, whose names are also given with those of the countries assigned to them (*ib.* xii. 1-8). Majjhantika was sent to

Kashmir and Gandhāra [cf. R.E. V.], Mahārakṣita to the Yavana country [mentioned in R.E. V. and XIII.; probably the same as the Greek kingdom of Bactria founded at this time in 246 B.C.], Majjhima to the Himālaya, Dharmarakṣita (a Yavana Buddhist) to Aparāntaka, Mahādharmarakṣita to Mahārāṣṭra (cf. Rāṣṭrikas of the Edicts), Mahādeva to Mahiṣamaṇḍala (the Satiyaputra country of the Edicts?), Rakṣita to Vanavāsī (north Kanara), Soṇa and Uttara to Suvarṇabhūmi (Pegu and Moulmein) and Mahendra with Riṣṭriya, Utriya, Sambala and Bhadrasāra to Laṅkā (Ceylon). That this information from the legends is trustworthy is proved by the fact that the names of some of these missionaries are found in some northern inscriptions. In a tope at Sāñchī was discovered a relic-urn, of which the inner lid had an inscription naming 'Majhima' and the outer lid naming 'Kāsapagota,' who, according to *Dīpavaṃsa* and *Mahābodhivaṃsa*, was the companion of Majjhima in his work in the Himālaya regions. The two names also occur on a relic casket from a tope at Sonārī with the designation Hemavatāchāriya, "teacher of the Himālaya region." Another relic-casket of the same place mentions Mogaliputa, probably the President of the Buddhist Council who organised the missions.

The remarkable point about these foreign missions of Asoka is that they were of the nature of welfare work among the peoples of other countries (such as supply of medical aid for the relief of suffering of both man and beast, as indicated in R.E. II.)., for which the Indian king provided the money out of his large-hearted liberality.

Now, what was the Dharma which Asoka was at such pains in introducing and spreading both in his own dominions and beyond? It comprised certain fundamental principles of thought and life, about which there can be no two opinions and which are acceptable and applicable to all mankind. In one edict [R.E. VII.] they are stated to be mastery of the senses (*samyama*), purity of thought (*bhāvaśuddhi*), gratefulness (*kṛitajñatā*) and steadfastness of devotion (*dṛidha-bhaktitā*); in another [P.E. II.], "little impiety, many good deeds, kindness (*dayā*), charity (*dāna*), truthfulness (*satya*) and purity in thought and deed (*śaucha*); and in a third edict [P.E. VII.], "dayā, dāna, satya, śau-cha, together with moda, *i.e.* blissfulness, and sādhutā or saintliness." But the Dharma was presented not merely in the form of doctrines, but in a more concrete form, for it must be lived and not merely believed, and that by the people at large, the masses, to whose average level of moral life it must adjust itself. Thus the basis of the Dharma was laid in the purity of domestic life, involving proper relations with "father and mother, kinsmen, servants and slaves, comrades, friends and supporters, seniors in age, the guru," the relations being analysed into those of service (śuśrūṣā), support (sampratipatti) or of reverence (*apachiti*) [R.E. III., IV. and IX.]. "The love that is kindled at home expands itself over the race of man." And so the next step in Asoka's religious scheme was to extend the circle of domestic affection so as to include Brāhmans and ascetics, homeless devotees, to whom all honour and liberality must be shown by the householders, as also lower animals depending on man.

On the basis of these practices was evolved a new ethics, which represents Asoka's contributions in the sphere of ideals. A separate edict was issued to emphasise Toleration as the essential element of religion in a land of many faiths. It was declared that "he who does reverence to his own sect while disparaging the sects of others wholly from attachment to his own, with intent to enhance the splendour of his own sect, in reality by such conduct inflicts the severest injury on his own sect;" for such a man lacks the essential of religion, viz. respect for "the essence of the matter that is in all sects," and a consequent "restraint of speech," considering that "the sects of other people all deserve reverence for one reason or another". Thus the emperor's special concern was that "there should be growth in the essence of the matter and respect for all sects," and not that his own sect and faith should flourish. He was himself the best example to his people of his own precept. He declared in his edict that "the king does reverence to men of all sects by gifts and various forms of reverence." As examples of Asoka's consideration for all sects may be mentioned his grant of cave-dwellings to the Ājīvikas, his enlargement of the stūpa of

Buddha Koṇāgamana on two occasions, his promotion of the interests of the Brāhmans, Ājīvikas, Nirgranthas, and various other sects equally with the Buddhists by the employment of his special officers, the Dharma-Mahāmātras [P.E. VII.], and his repeated insistence in the edicts on the duty of showing liberality to Brāhmans and Sramaṇas alike [R.E. III., IX.] and avoiding all unseemly behaviour to them [R.E. IV., P.E. VII.]. In his own tours through the country he made it a point of "visiting ascetics and Brāhmans with liberality to them" [R.E. VIII.], while by a special decree he removed the old established distinctions between different sects as regards rights of residence [R.E. VII.], declaring that "in all places men of every denomination may abide." Thus, in these edicts of Asoka, India, with the number and differences of her religions, has presented a conception of comparative and universal religion and a message of religious toleration centuries before the West could awake to them. Next to his message of Toleration may be mentioned that of the *True Ceremonial* specially applicable to Indian conditions. Among a people whose religion was so largely bound up with rituals, and moral life measured by the performance of 'various ceremonies in sickness, at weddings of sons and daughters, the birth of children, departure on journeys and on other similar occasions," the "many, manifold, trivial and worthless ceremonies" performed by the womankind, Asoka showed himself considerably ahead of his age in declaring that the True Ceremonial was the good and proper conduct in all relations of life, "proper treatment of slaves and servants, honour to teachers, gentleness towards living creatures and liberality towards ascetics and Brāhmans" [R.E. IX.]. The essence of religion was not ceremony, but character. On the same principle was also defined in another edict [R.E. XI] the *True Gift*, which was not the gift of goods, but of truth—the inculcation of Dharma and living it also in one's domestic and social relations. In another edict [R.E. IV.] he calls the inculcation of morals the best of deeds, for that is the first thing necessary to make a man moral. He has also emphasised self-exertion as the supreme need of moral life for "small and great" [M.R.E. I.],—"the utmost exertion, giving up all other aims," a need which is all the greater for a man of "high degree" [R.E. X.]. A method of this self-exertion is stated to be "self-examination," examination of one's bad deeds with his good ones [P.E. III.] or "reflection" [P.E. VII.], reflection on the Dharma, which helps one towards it more than its formal rules. Intense self-examination and intense efforts are thus pointed out as the aids to moral life [P.E. I].

It is thus clear that the Dharma or Religion as presented and preached in the edicts of Asoka is possessed of a universal appeal and applicability, and is more akin to a system of morals or ethics, which may be regarded as the common property of mankind and not the special possession of any particular sect. Thus Asoka had every justification in introducing it not only among his own subject-peoples irrespective of their creeds, but also in the foreign Hellenistic countries of the West, which he was anxious to bring into a line with the thought and life of India on account of their close connexion in many ways with India in that age. Nor should it be assumed that the message of Asoka, a message, essentially, of peace on earth and good-will among men, a message of Non-Violence (*ahiṃsā*), was in any way at all offensive to those foreign peoples in spite of their different religion and culture. And it is by such foreign missions that the Indian Buddhist thought has been able to influence Western thought in certain directions, as noticed in the heretical gnostic sects and certain orthodox forms of Christian teaching [V. Smith's *Early History*, 3rd ed., p. 188]. It may also be further noted that with such a universal scheme of religion and morality Asoka was justified in departing from the principle of neutrality which should ordinarily govern the religious policy of an emperor who has to deal with different creeds and communities. For by such a scheme he could show his positive and active interest in the moral and spiritual interests of his people, to the promotion of which he devoted the resources of his empire from his faith that it should be one of the primary concerns and cares of the state. In a special edict he has declared that the true glory and fame of a king do not rest upon the physical extent of his dominion, but upon the moral progress he can help his people to chieve [R.E. X.].

Lastly, along with the spheres of religion and morality, Asoka introduced certain very high ideals in the sphere of politics too. By his high moral purpose and earnestness, he moralised and spiritualised politics. The horrors of a single war convinced him that it was an absolute wrong and evil, which should have no place in his scheme of affairs. He forthwith gave effect to his conviction by declaring that "the chiefest conquest is the conquest of Right and not of Might" [R.E. XIII.]. A whole empire pledged itself to peace as an absolute good on its own initiative and inspiration without reference to its neighbouring states. The war-drum was completely silenced: the *bherī-ghoṣa* was no longer heard, but only the *dharma-ghoṣa* [R.E. IV]. The steam-roller of Mauryan aggression, which under Chandragupta had levelled down most of the independent states of India, was now brought to a halt: "Thus far and no farther" was Asoka's command. Many a small state or people in the remaining parts of India was spared its independence. India became a happy family of nations under an international system of Liberty, Equality and Fraternity for all, great or small. States unequal in size and strength were deemed equal as regards their status or sovereignty. The Yavanas, Kāmbojas and Gāndhāras on the north-western frontiers, the Nābhapantis, Bhojas, Andhras, Pulindas, Rāṣṭrikas and

Pitinikas in the central parts, and the Cholas and Pāṇḍyas, the Satiyaputras and Keralaputra in the south—all these small peoples were acclaimed by the emperor as his friends and equals in freedom, the objects not of a dreaded and forceful military conquest, but of his Moral Conquest, "Dharma-Vijaya" [R.E. XIII.], the objects of his tender solicitude for their spiritual welfare. Instead of sending an army to subdue them to his authority by violence, Asoka sent them his missionaries, *dūtas* [*ib*], to subdue them, by "a conquest full of delight," to the moral life he proposed for his own people. To the many unsubdued borderers of his empire was also sent the assuring message: "The king desires that they shoud not be afraid of him, but should trust him and should receive from him not sorrow, but happiness!" [K.E. I.]. The ruder folks too were not deemed unworthy of this message of love: "Even upon the forest folk His Majesty looks kindly" [R.E. XIII.]. Thus rang through the country, loud and clear, the healing message repeated on rock and pillar, the message of freedom, of peace on earth and goodwill among men. But there was one restriction in this Reign of Freedom. Freedom must not violate Morality. The sovereignty of Right enthroned in the place of Might must be maintained. While anxious "to secure the love and confidence of the borderers," Asoka was equally anxious "to set them moving on the path of piety" [K.E.I.]. The forest folks were warned not "to continue in their evil ways that they be not chastised" [R.E. XIII.]. Asoka thus stands out easily as the first of the peace-makers of the world. His moral conquests were successful not only in his own dominions, but also in some of the principal countries of the West, as stated by the emperor himself [R.E. XIII.].

His wide-hearted toleration and cosmopolitan catholicity were all the more remarkable for a man who was a zealous follower himself of a particular religion. For Asoka was a staunch Buddhist. He had all the sincerity and strenuousness of a new convert. Like his predecessors, he originally followed many practices not sanctioned by Buddhism. Animals were freely slaughtered in their thousands for the royal table every day "to make curries" (R.E. I.). He also used to indulge in all the customary merrymakings of kings before his definite adherence to Buddhism [R.E. VIII.]. The throne itself, according to tradition, he forcibly seized by killing the lawful heir, his eldest brother. And up to the eighth year of his coronation he was capable of waging a bloody war with the brave Kaliṅgas to extend his empire [R.E. XIII.].

He himself tells us the story of his conversion. He began as a mere lay-disciple, *upāsaka*, and continued as such "for more than two years and a half" without exerting himself strenuously for his progress in his new faith. Then he became involved in the Kaliṅga war and its carnage and cruelties, which, by a reaction, increased his faith in Buddhism, the religion of non-violence [M.R.E. I. and R.E. XIII.]. Then he entered the Order [*saṅgham upagata*, M.R.E. I.] not, as it may be assumed, as a full-fledged bhikṣu by taking the double ordination of *Pabbajja* and *Upasampada* as prescribed, but very probably as a *Bhikṣugatika*[1] [referred to in a passage of *Vinaya*, M., iii. 7, 8, S.B.E. tr.], which is the term applied to "a person who dwells in the same Vihāra with the Bhikkhus," but is not himself a Bhikṣu. Nowhere in any of the numerous legends about Asoka do we find any reference to his embracing monkhood by a formal renunciation of the world (*pravrajya*) and performing other ceremonies necessary for monkhood. Besides, the Saṅgha (as the *Vinaya*, M. i. 64 f shows) did not favour the admission of those who were under obligation of service to the state or would combine worldly duties with monkhood instead of proposing for themselves unmixed and lifelong monkhood. Thus, though Asoka was the greatest benefactor of the

[1] The *Mahāvaṃsa* relates how Asoka, then already known as Dharmāsoka by his unexampled benefactions to the Chruch, instead of himself taking orders, allowed his son and daughter to do so. By this his status in the Church was improved from that of *Pachchayadūyaku*, *i.e* an Upāsaka who supplied Bhikṣus with their four necessaries of food, clothing, shelter and medicine, to that of *Sāsanadāyāḍa*, *i.e.* a kinsman of the Church, a status which he himself carved for. Against this definite tradition, which represents Asoka as deliberately refraining from taking orders himself, it is absurd to find that fact in the edict [Geiger's tr., pp. 42-43].

The suggestion about the *Bhikṣugatika* I owe to Mr. Charandas Chatterji, M.A., Lecturer in my Department.

Saṅgha, he became so from the outside as king, and not from the inside as a monk.

The legends attribute his conversion to Buddhism to Nigrodha, his nephew, the son of his eldest brother, Sumana; to the preceptor, Moggali, identified with Upagupta of the northern tradition; but it was really due, as he himself states in his edict, to his remorse for the sin of the Kaliṅga War.

His progress in his new faith showed itself externally in some of his personal and public measures. He ordained [R.E.I.] that instead of "many hundred thousands of living creatures which were daily slaughtered to make curries in the royal kitchen, only three living creatures should be slaughtered, two peacocks and one antelope, the antelope not always." He also intended that "in future even these three creatures should not be slaughtered." Next, an ordinance was issued [P.E. V.] protecting specified animals and birds in different degrees; but it is significant that the peacock is not mentioned among them Buddhaghosa has in the *Samyutta Commentary* recorded that the peacock was a favourite article of food in the Majjhimadesa, which included Magadha! Another ordinance, more frankly Buddhist, prohibited the slaughter of *all* animals for sacrifice in the capital. It must have been felt as distinctly and directly aimed against popular Brāhmanical worship, in which sacrifice was an essential, an act of Asoka's intolerance and bigotry which is one of the few blots on his escutcheon! Asoka also kept his capital free of certain kinds of popular carnivals which were accompanied by animal fights, and excessive drinking, feasting and consumption of meat [R.E. I.]. In their place he introduced other kinds of popular amusements, more innocent and edifying, such as "shows and processions, exhibiting figures of the gods in their celestial cars, of sacred elephants, bonfires or illuminations, and many other divine spectacles" [R.E. IV]. His intention evidently was to educate the people by religious exhibitions, replacing the secular shows and military processions of his predecessors, which only corrupted the people's tastes and character. The same puritanical severity he applied to himself too. He would have none of the tours of pleasure, hunting and other similar amusements, so thoroughly enjoyed by all kings [R.E. VIII.]. He would instead have only "religious tours"—"visiting ascetics and Brāhmans with gifts to them, visiting elders with largess of gold, moving among his people, and holding religious conferences with them" [R.E. VIII.]. He would thus seek occasions of personal intercourse with his people to help them to a better life, and not his own sport or pleasure. Instead of the gay progresses of his predecessors, he would go on solemn pilgrimages to the Buddhist holy places. The edicts give us an indication of this pilgrimage in a passage [in R.E. VIII.] stating that "after he had been consecrated ten years he went out to

Bodh Gayā"[1] [*nikrami* (*ayāya* in Girnar version) *saṃbodhiṃ*, which is however usually interpreted to mean his progress towards enlightenment]. It may be noted that the emperor's visit to Bodh Gayā and its sacred tree is supposed by Foucher to be the subject of a sculpture on the eastern gate at Sāñchī. There are two other edicts bearing on his pilgrimage. The inscription on the Rummindei pillar, apparently the work of the local people, states that "when he had been consecrated twenty years, Asoka had come in person and paid homage to the sacred spot of Lumminī, where the Holy One was born." This pilgrimage was followed by the emperor's gift to the people of that village of freedom from religious cesses and fixing only one-eighth as land revenue. The other pilgrimage was to a place not connected with the Buddha, but to a previous Buddha, the stūpa of Koṇāgamana, which he also visited the same year as Lumbinī and had twice enlarged.

But a fuller account of his pilgrimage appears in literature and also in the record of the Chinese traveller, Yuan Chwang. Led by his guru, Upagupta of Mathurā, the son of the perfumer Gupta of Benares, the emperor, "escorted by a mighty army," started on a pilgrimage to all the chief holy places of Buddhism and thus visited Lumbinī Garden, where the Buddha was born, Kapilavastu, where he renounced the world, Bodh-Gayā where he became the Buddha, Ṛiṣipatana

[1] This meaning we owe to Prof. D. R. Bhandarkar of the Calcutta University.

(Sārnāth), where he first preached, Śrāvastī, where he mostly lived and taught and where were the stūpas of some of his chief disciples, Śāriputra, Maudgalyāyana and Ānanda, and, lastly, Kusinagara, where He attained his pari-nirvāṇa. Part of the route of the pilgrim's progress is marked by pillars on the royal road from Pātaliputra to the Nepalese tarai, the pillars at Bakhirā, Lauriyā-Ararāj (Radhiah), Lauriyā-Nandangarh (Mathiah) and Rāmpūrwā.

There were several other measures which mark him out to be a zealous Buddhist. He issued what is known as the Bhābrā or Second Bairāt Rock Edict, in which he speaks almost as the Head of the Church, specifying certain passages from the scriptures for recitation and meditation by the monks and nuns as well as the laity, male and female; and he also affirms his adherence to the Buddhist Trinity. In the Minor Pillar Edicts at Sārnāth, Kauśāmbī and Sāñchī he appears in a similar rôle as the Defender of the Faith, and fixes the penalties for the schismatics. Buddhaghosa has recorded that Asoka personally expelled some schismatics, "giving them white garments." He was also responsible for the third Buddhist Council held at Pāṭaliputra under th presidency of the famous Buddhist divine, Moggaliputta Tissa. The Council was convoked at a time of great confusion in the Church following the death of the two divines, Sumitra and Tissa, when heretics outnumbered the believers. The Council deliberated for nine months, and settled that the canon should be definitely closed, (after being defined in the treatise called *Kathavatthu*, produced by the President, in which the different opinions then prevailing are recorded. Lastly, the rather undue emphasis laid upon the sanctity of animal life as compared with human life, for which the only concessions of the emperor were the jail-deliveries on the anniversaries of his coronation, the reprieve of three days to convicts sentenced to death [R.E. V. and P.E. IV.] and appointment of special officers to prevent and nullify unjust imprisonment and torture [K.E. II. and R.E. V.], was probably due to his Buddhism. And the elaborate programme of his manifold public works for the comforts of man and beast and relief their suffering was evidently inspired by his personal religion.

We shall now consider what incidents and measures in Asoka's reign can be dated. In Rock Edict XIII. Asoka mentions as his contemporaries five Hellenic kings, from whose history it appears that they were all alive down to the year 258 B.C., when one of them died. Supposing for correctness of calculation that the news of his death took about a year to reach Asoka, we shall be safe in assigning to that edict the date of 257 B.C. As the edict was issued in the thitteenth year of his coronation, the date of his coronation would be 270 B.C., and, hence, that of his accession, 274 B.C.[1] The Kalinga War thus

[1] This date is that of the Purāṇas too, which assign to Chandragupta, who became king in about 323 B.C., a reign of 24 years, *i.e.* up to 299 B.C. and to Bindusāra, 25 years, *i.e.* up to 274 B.C.

took place in 262 B.C., immediately after which he became an earnest Buddhist, *i.e.* either a *Bhikkhugatika* or a *Sasanadayada*. After more than a year's earnestness in his new faith he issued the Minor Rock Edict I., which he thus must have done about 260 B.C. Before the conquest of Kalinga he was not an earnest Buddhist, but only an indifferent lay-disciple or *upasaka*, and this "for more than two years and a half" [M.R.E. I.], and so he first became an upāsaka, a convert to Buddhism, in about 265 B.C. Thus we get the following chronology for the recorded events of his reign:

274 B.C.—Accession at 21 (?).
270 B.C.—Coronation at 25 (?).
265 B.C.—Converted as an Upāsaka to Buddhism.
265-262 B.C.—Period of indifferent devotion to Buddhism.
262 B.C.—Kalinga War and increase of his faith in Buddhism; Asoka becomes a *Bhikkhugatika*.
260 B.C.—Issue of Minor Rock Edict I. after more than a year's strenuous devotion to Buddhism; his first "pious tour" [R.E. VIII.] and pilgrimage to Bodh-Gayā [*ib*]; addressing the Bhābrā Edict to the Church.
259 B.C.—Issue of the two Kalinga Edicts.
258-57 B.C.—Issue of the fourteen Rock Edicts in one corpus; grant of cave-dwellings to the Ājīvikas.
256 B.C.—Second enlargement of the stūpa of Koṇāgamana.

253 B.C.—Third Buddhist Council (?).

250 B.C.—Pilgrimage to Buddhist holy places; visit to the stūpa of Budha Koṇāgamana and erection of a commemorative pillar there.

243 B.C.—Issue of Pillar Edicts.

240 B.C.—Death of his queen, Asandhimitrā, and his marriage with Tiṣyarakṣitā (according to the legends).

237 B.C.—His death.

From this table of dates it would also appear that the various measures of Asoka which are referred to in his Rock Edicts (*e.g.* his Interdict of War, his Public Works, his Foreign Missions, etc.) must have been passed before the date of those edicts, *i.e.* between 260-58 B.C. (allowing at least two years' time for his foreign missions to achieve the success referred to in his Rock Edicts II. and XIII.), while the measures alluded to in the Pillar Edicts (*e.g.* Protection of Animals Act) were in operation before 243 B.C.

The edicts reflect the social conditions of the times. While domestic life called for the cultivation of proper relations with one's "father and mother, preceptor, kinsmen, servants and slaves, comrades, friends, supporters and elders." and was thus in its wide outlook and sympathies a valuable school of morality, the ascetic life seems to have been quite common and popular. The representative ascetic orders of the times are those of the Brāhmans, Buddhists or Śramaṇas, the Jains or Nirgranthas, and the Ājīvikas, besides other miscellaneous dissenting sects or pāṣaṇḍas not named in the edicts [cf. P.E. VII]. The Ājīvikas were given rock-cut cave-dwellings by the emperor (probably out of respect for his mother's connexion with them). The ascetics of different sects often met in debates and discussions on their respective doctrines, and a special edict enjoins upon them toleration, respect for the truth in each system, and restraint of speech in controversy [R.E. XII.]. The edicts voice social opinion in insisting on the duty of all householders to honour all ascetics, Brāhmans or Śramaṇas, irrespective of their creed. Buddhist ascetics were forward in social service. They were in charge of the foreign missions in Asoka's times. They were at work in the Himālaya country, in Suvarṇabhūmi, in Ceylon, and even "in the country of the Yona" [*Mahāvaṃsa*, xii. 6], probably the same as the five Hellenic countries of Syria, Egypt, Cyrene, Macedonia and Epirus mentioned in the edict. Hindu missionaries working in such distant countries solved the problem of foreign travel and sea-voyage. A notable proof of the width of social and religious outlook is furnished by the conversion of a Greek (Yona) into a Hindu and his appointment as an evangeliser of the Aparāntaka country [*Mahāvaṃsa* cited above]. Of a piece with this was the gift of a pillar in honour of Lord Vāsudeva in 140 B.C. by a Hindu Greek named Heliodorus, calling himself a Bhāgavata. The best thought of India has always touched the universal, overcoming all barriers, whether natural or artificial. Thus it spread to other lands and built up a greater India that was its pride and strength. The beginnings of this "expansion of India" are seen in Asoka's time. Lastly, we may note the considerable extent of literacy in the country, where the masses could read the edicts of Asoka written in their own dialects and scripts. Vincent Smith thinks that the percentage of litaracy in Asokan India must have been higher than it is now in many provinces of British India [*Asoka*, 3rd, ed., p. 139].

In conclusion, we shall note a few points about Asoka's personal life and family. Asoka does not give his name in his edicts, but only his titles, *Devānampiya* and *Piyadasi*. The former title was also taken by his predecessors [see R.E. VIII.] and also by his grandson, Daśaratha [see his inscription]. It was also used by his contemporary, Tissa, the king of Ceylon. The latter title in the form *Piadaṃsana* is given to Asoka's grandfather, Chandragupta, in the *Mudrārākṣasa*, (Act vi.). It was therefore difficult to connect the titles with Asoka till the difficulty was removed by the discovery of the Maskī Edict, which is not anonymous like all other edicts, but plainly uses the expression—*Devānaṃpiyasa Asokasa*. His personal name is, however, known to posterity. The Junāgaḍh inscription of Rudradāman (about 150 A.D.) uses the expression *Aśokasya Mauryasya* [*Ep. Ind.* vol. viii. p. 43]. A much later inscription, the Sārnāth Inscription of Kumāradevi [a queen of King Govinda Chandra of Kanouj (A.D. 1114-1154), *E.P. Ind.* vol. ix. p. 321], has the expression (v. 25) *Dharmā-śokanarādhipasya*, "of Dharmāśoka, the ruler of men." In the legends Asoka is generally called *Dharmāsoka* with reference to his piety and services to Buddhism, but they dub him as *Chaṇḍāsoka* before his conversion to Buddhism, with reference to his alleged cruelty in murdering his brothers (as many as 99) and thus wading through blood to the throne [*Mahāvaṃsa*, v. 189]. In the northern version of the legends, however, he is said to have murdered only one brother, his eldest, Prince Sumana or Susīma. If he had murdered any brothers, as the epithet *Chaṇḍāsoka* undoubtedly suggests, they might be his step-brothers. The edicts refer to the existence of his "brothers and sisters and other relatives" and their "female establishments" [R.E. V.], in whose welfare he is keenly interested. They also repeatedly insist on the cultivation of proper domestic relations in the joint family—which is against the theory that he was a fratricide. Fa-hien refers to a younger brother of Asoka who resided as an ascetic on a hill, but the king "begged him to come and live in his family, where he could supply all his wants," failing which he made him a hill in the city of Pāṭaliputra [Legge's tr., p. 77]. Here is another instance of Asoka's brotherly affection. The legends and the inscriptions together give us the names of the following relations of Asoka :—

Father—Bindusāra.

Mother—*Subhadrāṅgī*, daughter of a Brāhman of Champā (northern tradition); *Dharmā* [in the southern tradition (*Mahāvaṃsa-ṭīkā*, ch. v. p. 125[1]], whose family was a follower of the Ājīvika sect (whence probably Asoka's gifts of cave-dwellings to the Ājīvikas).

Brothers—Uterine and youngest brother called *Tiṣya* in Ceylon books and Vigatāśoka or Vītāśoka in northern tradition, and also Mahendra in some legends; eldest and step-brother, Sumana or Susīma.

Wives—(1) Devī of Vedisagiri in Ceylon books; (2) Kāruvākī, second queen, in the inscription; (3) Asandhimitrā; (4) Padmāvatī (*Divyāvadāna*, ch. xxvii.); and (5) Tiṣyarakṣita (*ib.*). Pillar Edict VII. refers to two classes of his wives, the queens called *Devīs*, whose sons are styled *Kumāras* and *Aryaputras* and others known from the designation of *dālaka* given to their sons.[2]

Sons—(1) Mahendra, whose mother was Devī; (2) Tīvara, son of Kāruvākī; (3) Kuṇāla, son of Padmāvatī (*ib.*); (4) Jalauka mentioned in the *Kashmir Chronicle*.

Daughters—Saṅghamitrā, whose mother was Devī; Chārumatī, who settled in Nepal.

Sons-in-law—Agni-Brahmā (husband of Saṅghamitrā) and Devapāla Kṣatriya, husband of Chārumatī.

Grandsons—Sumana, son of his daughter, Saṅghamitrā; Daśaratha; Samprati, son of Kuṇāla.

1 This passage was found for me by Mr. Charan Das Chatterji.

2 Bühler (Ep. Ind. II, p. 276) considers that the *devīkumārakāh* are the sons of the wives of Piyadasi's predecessors'.

SAMUDRAGUPTA

(330-375 A.D.)

WHILE Asoka stands for Peace and Non-violence, Samudragupta stands for the opposite principle of War and Aggression. The one had a contempt for conquests; the other had a passion for them. He was from the very first fired by the time-honoured ideal of a Kṣatriya king, which was to make himself the sovereign of the entire country up to its very ends and become a king of kings. In pursuit of this orthodox ideal set for a ruler, Samudragupta made out an elaborate programme of conquests in different directions (*digvijaya*) and realised it to a degree which has justly won him the title of an Indian Napoleon.

Lik Asoka, Samudergupta ha also left an account of his achievements. His various conquests of war and violence are detailed in an inscription engraved on the very same pillar which bears an inscription of Asoka telling of his different conquests of peace and piety! The emperor employed his poet laureate, named Hariṣeṇa, to compose a panegyric in Sanskrit in both verse and prose, in which were set forth all the exploits and glories achieved by his militarism.

The inscription describes Samudragupta as deceased, and was therefore engraved soon after his death by his successor, Chandragupta II. It is fond of referring to him as"the daughter's son of a Lichchhavi." We also gather that he was preferred for the throne by his father to all his brothers for his supeior qualifications. Some of these are thus described in the inscription :-"Who was skilful in engaging in a hundred battles of various kinds ; whose only ally was the prowess of the strength of his own arm ; whose most charming body was covered over with all the beauty of the marks of a hundred confused wounds caused by the blows of battle-axes, arrows, spears, pikes, barbed darts, swords, lances, javelins, iron arrows, and many other weapons." A hero of a hundred fights, he was able to make all parts of India acknowledge his paramount sovereignty by a victorious march through them continued for more than two or three years under the then physical conditions of such a march.

Firs , he "captured and liberated" a number of kings of the "Dakṣiṇāpatha" or South, viz. : "Mahendra of Kosala (in the valley of the Mahānadī), Vyāghrarāja of Mahākāntāra (one of the chiefs of the forest countries which still retain their ancient wildness and now constitute the tributary states of Orissa and the more backward parts of the Central Provinces) ; Mahendra of Piṣṭapura (modern Pithapuram) ; Svāmidatta of Koṭṭūra (Ganjam district) ; Maṇṭarāja of

Korāḷa (Kolleru lake[1]); Hastivarman of Veṅgī; Vishṇugopa of Kāñchī;[2] Ugrasena of Palakka[3] (either in Nellore district or Palghat); Damana of Eraṇḍapalla (Khandesh);[4] Nīlarāja of Avamukta; Kubera of Devarāṣṭra (Mahārāṣṭra);[5] Dhanañjaya of Kusthalapura, and other kings."

[1] Jouveau-Dubreuil, in his *Ancient History of the Deccan* (pp. 58-61), vigorously protests against some of these identifications of Fleet, and maintains that Samudragupta's conquests were confined only to the *east* coast of the Deccan and were not carried either to the south or to the west of the Deccan. Thus he identifies *Kaurāla* of the inscription with the Korāla kingdom.

[2] In his book on *The Pallavas* (pp. 14, 15) Jouveau-Dubreuil shows that, as the Pallavas held a dominion extending up to the Kṛiṣṇā, it was not necessary for Samudragupta to give battle to their king, Viṣṇugopa, at his capital at Kāñchī. The two kings must have met on, or a little northward of, the banks of the Kṛiṣṇā. Thus the area of Samudragupta's conquests is, in this view, considerably reduced.

[3] According to Jouveau-Dubreuil a capital to the south of the Kṛiṣṇā mentioned in many Pallava copper-plates [*JRAS*, 1905, p. 29].

[4] Identified by Jouveau-Dubreuil with a town near Chicacole in Ganjam district, called Eraṇḍapali and referred to in the Siddhāntam plates of Devendravarman [*Ep. Ind.* vol. xiii. p. 212].

[5] According to Jouveau-Dubreuil (*Ancient History*, p. 60), an old province in the district of Vizagapatam. "A set of copper-plates discovered in 1908-9 at Kāsimkoṭa in the district of Vizagapatam mentions the grant by the E. Chalukyan king, Bhīma I., of a village situated in Elamañcha Kalingadeśa (modern Yella-manchili) Kalingadeśa, a part of the province called Devarāshṭra" [No. 59 of *Madras Epigraphy Report for* 1908-9].

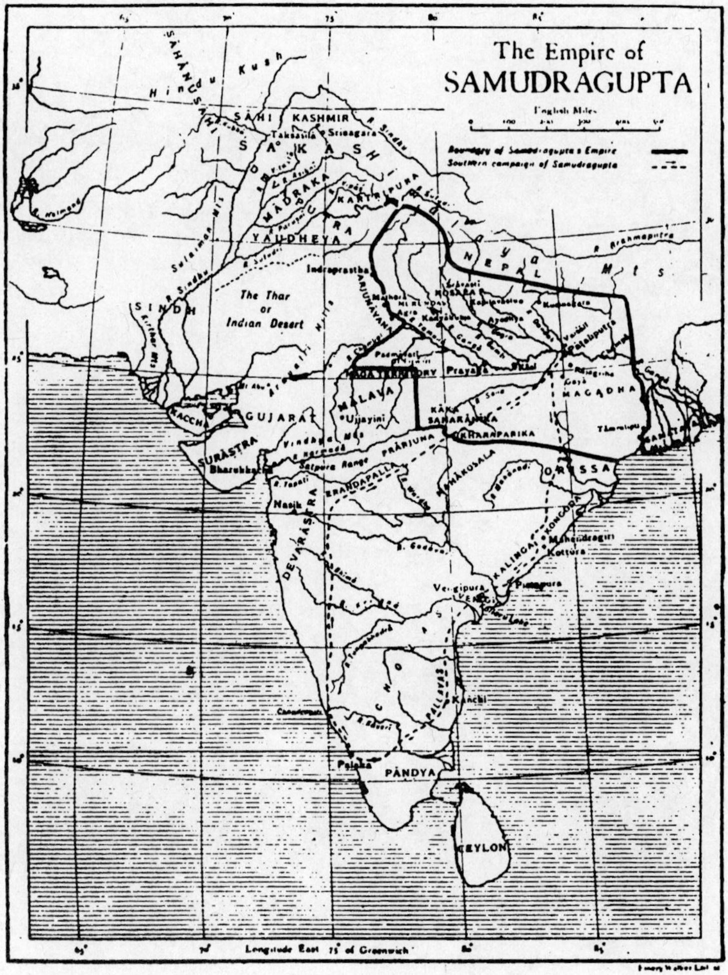

The Empire of
SAMUDRAGUPTA
English Miles
Boundary of Samudragupta's Empire
Southern campaign of Samudragupta
Hindu Kush
KASHMIR
Takasila
Srinagara
MADRAKA
KARTRIPURA
YAUDHEYA
Indraprastha
NEPAL
The Thar
or
Indian Desert
SINDH
ARJUNAYANA
Mathura
Agra
KOSALA
Ayodhya
Pataliputra
Prayaga
MAGADHA
Gaya
MALAVA
Ujjayini
GUJARAT
KACCHA
SURASTRA
Bharukkacha
Satpura Range
PRARJUNA
SAHARANIKA
KHARAPARIKA
ORISSA
MAHAKOSALA
ERANDAPALLA
Nasik
DEVARASTRA
KALINGA
KONGODA
Mahendragiri
Kottura
Vengipura
VENGI
Pistapura
PALLAVAS
Kanchi
PANDYA
CEYLON
Longitude East 75° of Greenwich

Next, he "violently exterminated" the following kings of Āryāvarta, Uttarāpatha, or the North, who were his neighbours, at whose expense his empire had to extend: "Rudradeva, Matila, Nāgadatta, Chandravarman, Gaṇapati-Nāga, Nāgasena, Achyuta, Nandin, Balavarman and many other kings." Of these names only one, that of Gaṇapati-Nāga, has been identified as the king whose capital was at Padmāvatī or Narwār, a city still existing in the Gwalior State.

Thirdly, he reduced to the condition of serfdom (literally, his servants, *parichāraka*) all the kings of the "forest-countries" (supposed by Fleet to be in Central India).

Fourthly, the frontier states both in the east and in the west also submitted to him "by giving all kinds of taxes, obeying his orders and tendering homage." These states in the east were the kingdoms of Samataṭa (the delta of the Ganges and Brahmaputra), Kāmarūpa (Assam), Davāka (modern Bogra, Dinajpur and Rajshahi districts), Kartṛipura (identified with Kumaon, Almora, Garwāl and Kāṅgrā), Nepal and other countries. The states in the west were not kingdoms, but republics of peoples called "Mālavas, Ārjunāyanas, Yaudneyas, Mādrakas, Abhīras, Prārjunas, Sanakānīkas, Kākas, Kharaparikas and others."

As a result of all these conquests, Samudragupta "had no antagonist of equal power in the world," "by whom the whole tribe of kings upon the earth was overthrown and reduced to the loss of the wealth of their sovereignty" [Erān Stone inscription].

His conquests in their wide range were necessarily of different degrees. The inscription shows that there were (*a*) kings who were killed and whose dominions were annexed to Samudragupta's empire; (*b*) kings who were defeated, taken prisoners and then liberated and reinstated as his vassals; (*c*) the frontier states, kingdoms and republics, which anticipated his conquest by offering submission and personal homage to the emperor beforehand.

Samudragupta was not, however, a ruthless annexationist, but a magnanimous, conqueror, generous towards the fallen foe. "His fame, which pervades the whole world, is due to his re-establishing many royal families whom he had overthrown and deprived of sovereignty."

Thus Samudragupta made himself the master of a wide empire extending in the east to the Brahmaputra, in the south to the Narmadā and in the north up to the Himālayas and Kashmir. But wider than the sphere of his direct dominion and authority was the sphere of his influence and suzerainty, the range of his international alliances and relations. We learn from a Chinese historian that King Meghavarman of Ceylon (352-79 A.D.) deputed two monks, one of whom is stated to have been his brother, to Bodh-Gayā to see Asoka's monastery to the east of the sacred tree there and pay homage to the Diamond Throne. The strangers, meeting with scant courtesy there, returned and induced the king to make arrangements for the proper accommodation of his subjects going on pilgrimage to India. For this purpose he sent a formal embassy with the gifts of gems and other precious articles for which Ceylon was noted to the Indian emperor, who at once granted permission to build a monastery near the sacred tree. The King of Ceylon built a monastery of three stories, six halls and three towers, enclosed within a wall 30 or 40 feet high. Inside were decorations of painting and a statue of the Buddha of gold and silver, studded with gems of various colours. The establishment is called Mahābodhi Saṅghārāma by Yuan Chwang, who saw it accommodating nearly "1000 ecclesiastics, all Mahāyānists of the Sthavira school" [Watters, ii. 136]. Thus the King of Ceylon was anxious to be on good terms with Samudragupta. Probably the fact of this embassy from Ceylon sent to him with presents is pointed to in the inscription by the expression—"bringing gifts from the people of Siṃhala and all the dwellers in the islands.".

Towards the north-west his influence extended into distant regions. Some of these peoples may have been actually defeated in war by Samudragupta, considering that they were so anxious to be in his good graces. To such cases of submission to his suzerainty the inscription thus refers: "Whose binding together of the whole world by his strong arm was effected by the acts of homage, such as self-sacrifice, the bringing of gifts of maidens, the soliciting of charters confirming them in the enjoyment of their territories" [Allan's *Catalogue of Indian Coins*, p. xxiv], while the parties rendering such homage are named "Daivaputras, Ṣāhis, Ṣāhānuṣāhis, Śakas and Murunḍas." Of these names, the first three are titles, and not ethnics like the last two. They were the titles originally adopted by the great Kushān emperors Kaniṣka, Huviṣka and Vāsudeva. By the third and fourth century A.D. the Kushān empire was disintegrated into a number of smaller states, whose rulers divided among themselves these titles according to their status. The title of *Ṣāhi* was adopted by one branch of the Kushān race, the Kidāra Kushāns. The title *Ṣāhi-Sāhānuṣāhi* is the Iranian title for the suzerain or king of kings, and should refer to a great king outside India, whom Vincent Smith identifies with the Sassanian emperor, Sapor II., who actually used that title. But Allan identifies him with the great king of the Kushāns, "whose kingdom stretched from the Indian borders to the Oxus," on the ground that "there is no evidence of intercourse between the Gupta and Sassanian empires at this period, while we know that there was a powerful kingdom between them." It is difficult to say who is actually meant by the title *Daivaputra*, which is the Indian equivalent of the Chinese imperial title meaning "son of heaven," and was borrowed by the Kushān emperors from the Chinese, just as the other title *Ṣāhānuṣāhi* was inherited by them from the Scythian rulers of Bactria and India. Kennedy supposed that the "Devaputra of India," as mentioned by

Chinese historians, meant a ruler of the Punjab, whose country is referred to by them as famous for its elephants [*ibid.* p. xxvii.]

As regards the *Śakas*, they may include the Western Kṣatrapas of Saurāṣtra, up to whose frontiers. extended the conquests of Samudragupta so as to pave the way for his son's conquest of their kingdom. But there were other Śakas in the north who "issued coins of Kushān types which formed the prototypes of Samudragupta's coinage" [*ib.* p. xxvii], and these Śakas may have been meant in the inscription.

"The fact that Samudragupta's coins are strongly influenced by those of the Kushān kings of the Panjab, and seem quite uninfluenced by those of the Kushan kings of Kabul, is perhaps evidence that his arms did not penetrate so far" [*ib.*].

The *Muruṇḍas* are mentioned among the races of foreign origin which ruled in India and are mentioned along with the Śakas, Yavanas and Tukhāras in the Purāṇas. Some Jain books refer to a Marundarāja as ruler of Kanyākubja and resident of Pāṭaliputra; while Ptolemy [vii. 2, 14] probably refers to the Muruṇḍas as living on the left bank of the Ganges. There is a Chinese record of the third century A.D. which refers to a king of a country in India under the name *Meon-lou* [*ib.* xxix]. Thus the Gupta empire probably rose on the ruins of the Murundas.

Thus the suzerainty of Samudragupta was recognised over a wide area extending from

Ceylon through the territory of the Devaputra and the Śakas of the Panjab, the Ṣāhi Kushāns of Gandhāra and the Ṣahānuṣāhis of Kabul right up to the Oxus.

Samudragupta also took steps to have his suzerainty formally proclaimed by reviving the institution of horse-sacrifice, which had fallen into abeyance in the long period of about 400 years after the Śuṅga emperor, Puṣyagupta, during which there did not appear any ruler in India to achieve the status of an emperor and claim to perform the ceremony appropriate for it. There are still to be seen some of the gold coins struck on the occasion to be distributed as gifts among Brāhmans. They show a figure of the horse to be sacrificed before an altar and the legend—"the Mahārājādhirāja of irresistible valour having conquered the earth now wins heaven (*i.e.* by sacrifice, etc.)." The reverse of the coins shows the figure of the queen, assigned an important part in the sacrifice, and the legend *Aśvamedha-parākramaḥ*, "he whose supremacy has been established by the Aśvamedha." The same sacrifice is supposed to be indicated by a stone figure of a horse found in Oudh and now in the Lucknow Museum, which bears an incomplete Prākṛit legend "*—ddaguttassa deyadhaṃma.*"

Much of the history of his career is told by his coins, which remarkably confirm the information supplied by the inscriptions. The various types of Samudragupta's coinage are distinguished as: (1) Standard; (2) Archer; (3) Battle-axe; (4)

Chandragupta I.; (5) Kācha; (6) Tiger; (7) Lyrist; and (8) Aśvamedha. Except the types (6) and (7), all the other coin-types bear legends indicative of Samudragupta's conquests and his consequent attainment of paramount sovereignty. On coins belonging to type No. 1 the full legend obtained by piecing together the fragments on individual coins reads—"Samaraśatavitatavijayo jitaripur ajito divaṃ jayati," which means "the unconquered one whose victories extend over a century of battles, having conquered his enemies, wins heaven." The full legend on the second type is—"Apratiratho vigitya kṣitiṃ sucharitair divaṃ jayati," *i.e.* "having conquered the earth, the invincible one wins heaven by good deeds" (probably sacrifices, but not the horse-sacrifice, as this type of coins seems to be earlier than the Aśvamedha type). The third or Battle-axe type bears as the complete legend, not found on any single coin, the following—"Kṛitānta-paraśur jayaty-ajitarājajetājitaḥ," "wielding the axe of Kṛitānta, the unconquered conqueror of unconquered kings is victorious." Here he is likened to Yama, the god of death, whose power is irresistible. In the Allahabad and Erāṇ inscriptions is compared to Antaka (another name of Yama), whom he resembles in anger according to the latter. The Kācha type has the legend—"Kācho gām avajitya divaṃ karmabhir uttamair jayati," Kācha having conquered the earth wins heaven by the highest works", while the reverse legend is *Sarvarājochchhetā*, "exterminator of all the kings."

Thus all these coins of various types were issued after the completion of his full programme of conquests. This is declared not only by their legends, but also by their make. The first five types of Samudragupta's coinage are in the opinion of numismatists based upon the later Kushān coinage, from which are borrowed the following features, viz. (*a*) writing the king's name vertically as in the Standard type; (*b*) retaining the meaningless traces of the back of the throne on the reverse in imitation of the Kushān coinage, which shows on the reverse the goddess Ardokhṣo (AP∆OXPO) on a high-backed throne; and (*c*) giving to the king the Kushān dress with slight variations. Samudragupta thus modelled his own coinage on the coins of the later Kushān kings only after he had made them submit to his suzerainty. Later in his reign he issued the other types of coins which show his originality and independence of Kushān models. Both on the Tiger and the Lyrist type there is hardly any trace of Kushān influence in the king's attitude or dress; "except for his jewellery he is naked to the waist; on some specimens the Kushān peaked headdress is replaced by a tight-fitting cap, but on others he is distinctly bare-headed," while on the reverses the goddess Lakṣmi is seen in her indigenous form and pose and not like Ardokhṣo.

But Samudragupta was noted not more for his conquests than for his proficiency in the humanities of the times, his literary and artistic achievements.

STONE FIGURE OF A HORSE, SUPPOSED TO BE THAT SACRIFICED BY SAMUDRAGUPTA.
(By the courtesy of the Curator Lucknow Provincial Museum)

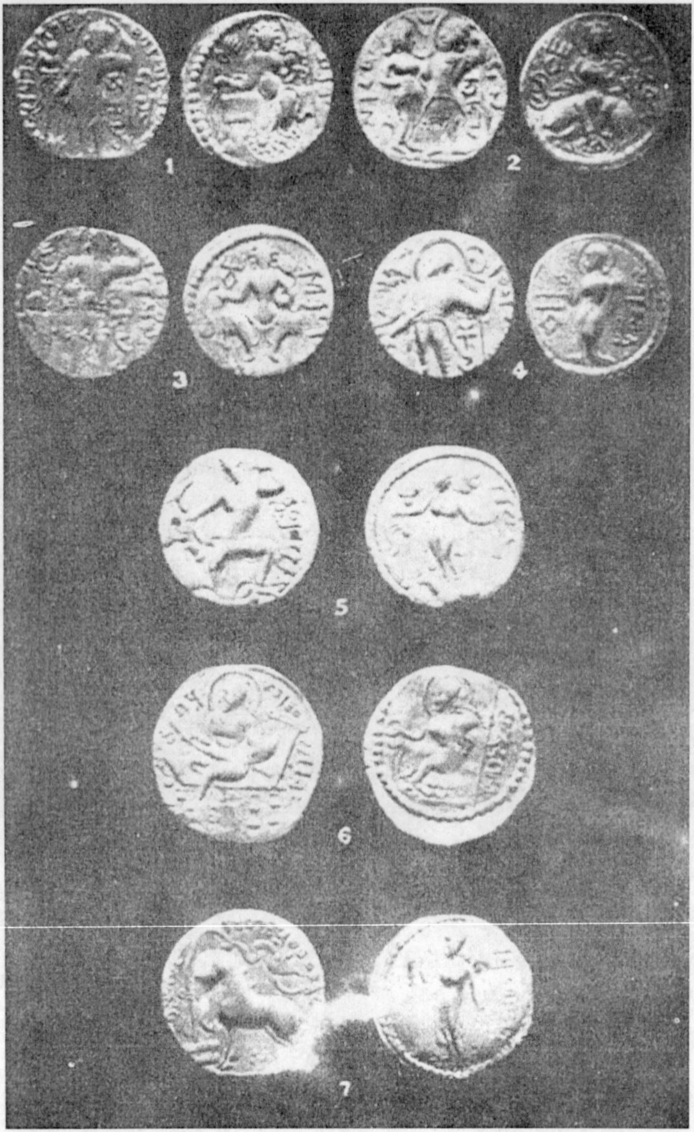
1
2
3
4
5
6
7

GOLD COINS OF SAMUDRAGUPTA (A. D. 335-80).

(From casts supplied by the courtesy of the Curator of the Provincial Museum, Lucknow.)

1 STANDARD TYPE.

Obv. King standing to left, nimbate, wearing close-fitting cap, coat and trousers, earrings and necklace, holding in left hand standard, dropping incense on altar with his right hand; on left, behind altar, a standard bound with fillet and surmounted by a Garuḍa facing.

Beneath king's arm, on either side of standard in two vertical rows, *sa-mu-dra* || *gu-pta*. Portions of legend starting from right, *Samaraśatavitatavijayo jitaripurajito divaṁ jayati.*

Rev. Goddess (Lakṣmī) seated facing on a four-legged throne, nimbate, wearing loose robe, necklace and armlets, holding fillet in outstretched right hand and cornucopiae in left arm; feet resting on lotus.

Symbol to left, to right traces of *Parākramaḥ*:

2. IN COMMEMORATION OF THE MARRIAGE OF CHANDRAGUPTA I. AND KUMĀRADEVĪ.

Obv. Chandragupta I. standing to left offering some object to Kumāradevī who stands on left to right; both nimbate; the King holding in left hand a crescent-topped standard.

Legend on right, on either side of the standard, *Chandra-gupta*; on left, *Kumāradevī*.

Rev. Goddess (Lakshmī) seated facing a lion couchant to right. To left symbol, and to right, *Lichch bavayaḥ*.

3. BATTLE-AXE TYPE.

Obv. King, nimbate, standing to left, holding battle-axe in left hand; on left a boy behind whom is a crescent-topped standard.

On either side of battle-axe, *Samudra* || *gupta*, and beginning right...*rājajetājitaḥ*.

Rev. Goddess (Lakṣmī) seated on a couch; on left, symbol; on right, *Kṛi-tā-nta paraśuḥ*.

4. Kacha Type.

Obv. King standing to left, holding standard surmounted by wheel in left hand and sprinkling incense on altar with right hand. Beneath left arm, *Kācha*; legend beginning right *Kācho gāmava... karmabhir uttamair jayati.*

Rev. Goddess standing to left, nimbate. To right *Sarvarājochchhettā*. Symbol on left.

5. Tiger Type.

Obv. King shooting tiger with bow and trampling on it when it falls backwards.

On right *Vyāghraparākramaḥ*.

Rev. Goddess (*Gaṅgā*) standing left on *makara*, holding lotus in left hand. Crescent-topped standard bound with fillet to left. No symbol. On right, *Rājā Samudragu(ptaḥ.)*

6. Lyrist Type.

Obv. King seated on couch with left leg pendent and resting on footstool and the right drawn up. He plays on a *Vīṇā* or lute placed on his knees. Legend beginning right *Mahārājādhirāja Śrī Samudraguptaḥ*.

Rev. Goddess (Lakṣmī) seated to left on wicker stool, holding fillet and cornucopiae in right and left hands respectively. On right, *Samudraguptaḥ*.

7. Aśvamedha Type.

Obv. Horse standing left before sacrificial post (*yūpa*) from which pennons fly backwards. Beneath horse, *Si*. Legend starting right, *Rājādhirājaḥpṛithivīṁ vijitya...*

Rev. Chief queen (Mahiṣī) standing left, holding chowrie over right shoulder, left hand hanging by her side; on left is the sacrificial spear bound with fillet. No symbol. On right, *Aśvamedhaparākramaḥ*.

[The descriptions of the coins are based on those of Allan in his *Catalogue of Indian Coins* (Gupta Dynasties).]

Ample evidence for this is furnished both by the inscriptions and the coins. The Allahabad Pillar inscription describes how he was well versed in the Śāstras [line 5, *śāstra-tattv-ārthabharttuḥ*, lines 15 and 30]; how, himself a learned man, he was fond of the company of learned men (l. 5). But his learning was not confined to the sacred lore alone. He was the prince of poets (*Kavirāja*, l. 27), whose "various poetical compositions were fit to be the means of subsistence of learned people" (l. 27) and gave him an empire of fame for his enjoyment [*Kīrttirājyam bhunakti*, l. 6]. He was master of "that true poetry which gives free vent to the power of the mind of poets" l. 16.). Altogether "his sharp and polished intellect put to shame Kaśyapa, the preceptor of Indra" (l. 27). Besides poetry, he also cultivated the sister art of music. He "put to shame Nārada by his choral skill and musical accomplishments" (*gāndharva-lalitaiḥ*, l. 27). The *Lyrist Type* of his coins represents Samudragupta seated on a high-backed couch, cross-legged to left, wearing waist-cloth, close-fitting cap, necklace, ear-rings and armlets, and playing on the lyre or lute (vīṇā) which lies on his knees, while below the couch is a pedestal or footstool. Some coins represent him bareheaded and thus more at ease.

His cultivation of these softer arts of poetry and music was combined with that of the sterner arts of the warrior. He depicts himself as an archer on some of his coins (type No. 2 above), which represent him as holding a bow in his left hand and an arrow in his right with the head of the arrow resting on ground. On other coins he stands out as the invincible hunter and takes the title *Vyāghra-parākrama*, of which the meaning is visible on the obverse, representing the king as trampling on a live tiger, which falls back as he shoots it. Wearing only waist-cloth, turban and some jewellery, he stands as the very picture of energy.

Ruthless towards his enemies, he was kind towards his own people. A warm heart was always beating under his coat of mail. The inscription describes how, "being full of compassion, he had a tender heart that could be won over simply by devotion and obeisance" (l. 25). Forgiving to the fallen foe, "he always employed his officers to restore the wealth of the various kings who had been conquered by the strength of his arms" (l. 26). Regarding his own subjects, "he was the very incarnation of kindness, whose mind busied itself with the support of the miserable, the poor, the helpless and the afflicted" (*ib.*). He is also spoken of as "the giver of many hundreds of thousands of cows" (l. 25). The Eraṇ inscription speaks of his gift of gold pieces (*suvarṇa-dāna*) evidently in connexion with his horse-sacrifice.

We have some details of his personal life in some of the inscriptions of his successors [*e.g.* the Bilsaḍ, Bihār and Bhitarī Stone Pillar inscriptions of Kumāragupta and Skandagupta, as well as the spurious Gayā Copper-plate inscription ascribed to Samudragupta]. His great grandfather was Gupta, grandfather Ghaṭotkacha, father Chandragupta, mother Kumāradevī the Lichchhavi princess, and his wife Mahādevī Dattadevī. On his coins of the Aśvamedha type apears the figure of his chief queen (mahiṣī) without her name, in loose robes and bejewelled, holding a chowrie over her right shoulder in her right hand. The Chandragupta type of coins represents his father and mother, the father holding a crescent-topped standard and offering to his mother a wedding ring or bracelet. The father wears close-fitting coat, trousers and headdress, ear-rings and armlets, while his wife is in loose robes, wearing ear-rings, necklace, armlets and tight-fitting headdress.

It is interesting to note that the inscriptions mentioned above sum up his achievements by applying to him some standing epithets : "The exterminator of all kings, without a rival in the world, whose fame was known as far as the four oceans, the equal of Dhanada, Varuṇa, Indra and Antaka, armed with the axe of Kṛitānta himself, the giver of many cows and koṭīs of gold pieces out of his lawfully acquired abundance and the reviver of the long lost ceremony of horse-sacrifice."

His coins tell us something about his religion. The crescent-topped standard associated with his father is replaced by the Garuḍa standard. Garuḍa, the bird and vehicle of Viṣṇu, thus became the badge of the Gupta emperors. In the Allahabad inscription we have mention of kings of the north asking for "charters bearing the Garuḍa seal," which thus came to be the personal seal of Samudragupta. His son and successor, Chandragupta II., calls himself a Bhāgavata, probably a Vaiṣṇava. But his Vaiṣṇavism was not inconsistent with militarism, which should mark a Kṣatriya according to the teachings of the *Bhagavad-gītā*. There is some evidence to show that the king came under the influence of Buddhism through its great apostle Vasubandhu in his early life. The rhetorician Vāmana (*c.* A.D. 800) refers to a son of Chandragupta as a patron of men of letters and calls him by the name of Chandraprakāśa, while as an instance of his literary patronage the commentator refers to Vasubandhu being appointed minister of the youthful king. The youthful king was in all probability no other than Samudragupta, who must have then at least two other names, viz. Kācha and Chandraprakāśa (*i.e.* moon in full glory, as contrasted with Chandragupta, under whom the Gupta power was not full grown). Secondly, in Paramārtha's *Life of Vasubahdhu* it is stated that King Vikramāditya of Ayodhyā, who had leanings towards the Sāṅkhya philosophy, was induced by Vasubandhu to take interest in Buddhism and appoint him as tutor to his son Bālāditya. When the latter became king he brought Vasubandhu to Ayodhyā and showed him special favours. Since Vasubandhu is said to have lived and died in the fourth century A.D. [Macdonell's

Sanskrit Literature, p. 325], Baladitya must be another name for Samudragupta. That Ayodhyā was one of the principal cities of his empire is evident from the spurious Gayā Copper-plate inscription which mentions Ayodhyā as one of the victorious camps of Samudragupta, "full of great ships, elephants and horses." Yuan Chwang also repeats the tradition connecting Vasubandhu with a Vikramāditya, King of Śrāvastī, who "reduced the Indies to submission," by which Samudragupta is evidently meant. Lastly, the date of Vasubandhu tallies with that of Samudragupta [see App. N, V. Smith's *Early History*, pp. 328 f.]. Probably we owe to Samudragupta's association with Vasubandhu the catholicity which made him welcome the proposal of the Buddhist King of Ceylon to build for pilgrims from his country a monastery at Bodh-Gayā, as related above.

HARSHA

(606-647 A.D.)

HARṢA combines in himself some of the attributes and characteristics of both Samudragupta and Asoka. By his thorough-going conquests in different directions, recalling the military idealism of Samudragupta, he first won for himself the status of an emperor and recovered for the country the unity of its history, which was lost in local annals. And then, making an end of all wars within his empire politically united by the strong arm of his authority, he proceeded, like Asoka, to devote himself to the tasks of peace, the promotion of the material and moral interests of the country, and to bring out her cultural individuality and greatness.

Harṣa's wars were, however, not those of unmotived aggression, but wars of vengeance. The political position of India was then one of unstable equilibrium. The break-up of the Gupta empire led to the rise of many petty states, whose mutual dissensions invited the Hūṇas to renew their raids in the north. The situation called for a sovereign who could act up to the time-honoured Kṣatriya ideal of bringing the entire country under the umbrella of one authority. Harṣa's father, King Prabhākaravardhana of Sthāṇvīśvara, well-nigh realised this ideal: he made his power felt by the Hūṇas, the kings of the Indus land and Gandhāra, by the lawless Lāṭs, in Gujarat and Malwa [Bāṇa's *Harṣa-charita*,[1] 133] and won for himself the title of Pratāpaśīla. But he died in the midst of his campaigns against the Hūṇas, against whom he had despatched the Crown Prince Rājyavardhana with an immense force and attended by his ancient advisers and devoted feudatories (166). The younger brother, Harṣa, also followed him with a cavalry force, and was hunting in the northern hills when the news of his father's illness delivered to him by the messenger, Kuraṅgaka, made him hurriedly ride back to the capital only to see his father pass away and his mother, Queen Yaśovatī, dying before her husband as a Satī (187). Prince Rājyavardhana returns after conquering the Hūṇas; but, before the tears on his eyes for his departed father had time to dry up, he received the heart-rending news of his sister, Rājyaśrī, being widowed by the murder of her husband, the Maukhari king, Granavarman, by the King of Mālwa, who kept

[1] The translation of the work by Messrs. Cowell and Thomas I have throughout used in this chapter.

her in fetters at Kanyākubja! This made the new king march at once against the murderer of Mālwa, leaving behind Harṣa, much against his protestations, in charge of the capital. But misfortune never comes singly! Kuntala, the chief cavalry officer of Rājyavardhana, delivers to Harṣa the news that his brother, after routing the Mālwa army with ease, has been led into a trap by the King of Gauḍa, Śaśāṅka, and murdered. Thus a war of vengeance was forced upon Harṣa. The Council of Ministers, who called him to the vacant throne, led by the old Commander-in-chief Siṃhanāda, advised Harṣa not only to chastise the Gauḍa king, but to end the system which might breed such treachery and trouble, the system of petty warring states in the country. Thus Harṣa starts on a "conquest of the four quart ," and a proclamation to that effect was issued by Avanti, the Prime Minister. In the meanwhile Bhaṇḍi, his cousin, who had followed his brother in his war against Mālwa, re with the spoils of victory, including the w e Mālwa army, elephants, horses and treasure, and delivers the news that Princess Rājyaśrī had escaped from the prison at Kanyākubja into the wilds of the Vindhyas. The first march of Harṣa is therefore towards the Vindhan forests, where with the help of the forest chiefs Vyāghraketu, Nirghāta, and Bhūkampa and the Buddhist hermit Divākaramitra, and his disciples, he was able to recover in the nick of time his widowed sist from the flames in which she was about to

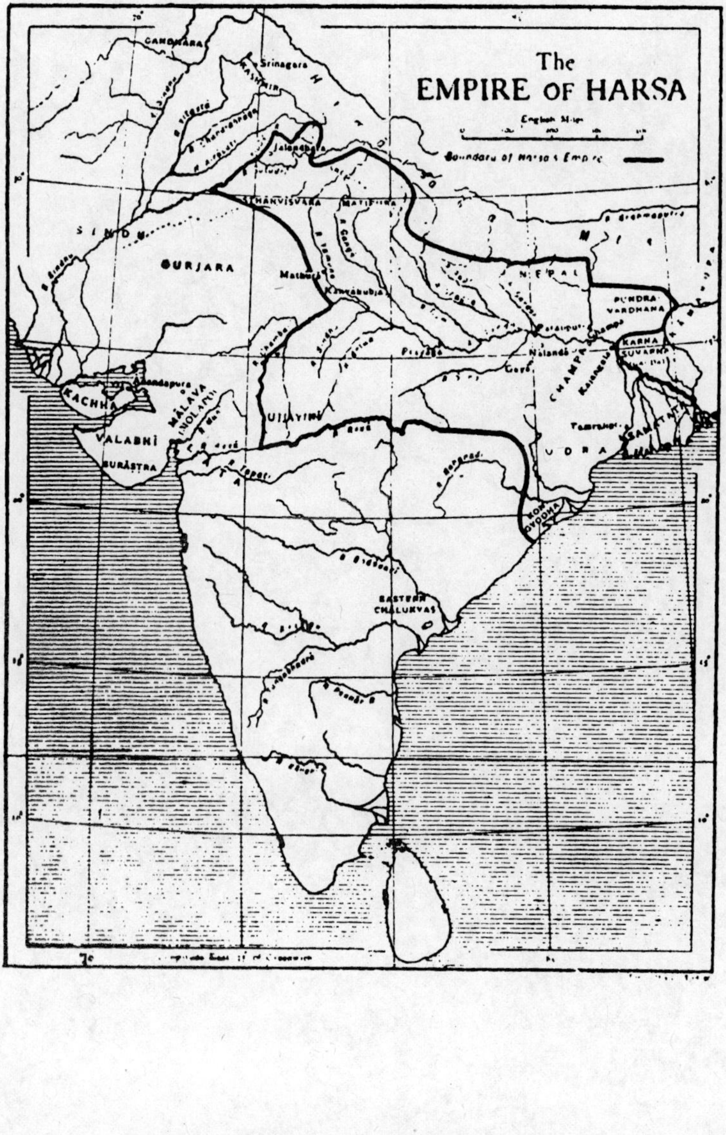

The
EMPIRE OF HARSA
Boundary of Harsa's Empire
GANDHARA
Srinagara
KASHMIR
Jalandhara
STHANVISVARA
MATHURA
SINDHU
GURJARA
Mathura
Kanyakubja
NEPAL
PUNDRA VARDHANA
Pataliputra
Nalanda
Champa
Gaya
Prayaga
KARNA SUVARNA
CHAMPA
UJJAYINI
Anandapura
KACHHA
MĀLAVA
VALABHĪ
SURĀSTRA
Tamralipti
SAMATATA
UDRA
KONGODA
EASTERN CHALUKYAS

sacrifice herself as a Satī. Under the influence of the Buddhist saint both the brother and the sister felt drawn towards Buddhism ; but Harṣa decided that they would "assume the red garments together" (288) after he had accomplished his vow of vengeance and the conquests upon which he had already embarked.

With an army of 5000 elephants, 20,000 cavalry, and 50,000 infantry, he "proceeded eastwards, invaded the states which had refused allegiance an waged incessant warfare until in six years he had brought the Five Indies under allegiance," as Yuan Chwang informs us [Watters, i. 343]. The "Five Indies" are stated to be Savārāṣṭra (Panjab), Kanyāubja, Gauḍa (Bengal), Mithilā and Orissa. The details of all the conquests of Harṣa are not known. According to Bāṇa, he seems to have subdued Sindh and a land of snowy mountains (probably Nepal), while the King of Assam sought his alliance from the beginning. In the west 'he reduced the kingdom of Valabhai, which then included Mo-la-po, the name given by Yuan Chwang to Western Mālava, together with its dependencies, Ānandapura, Ki-ta (Cutch ?) and Su-la-cha (Surat). The King of Valabhi, Dhruvasena II. or Dhruvabhaṭṭa [Watters, ii. 246], at first sought the protection of the Gurjara king, Dadda II., a feudatory of the suzerain of the south, Pulikeśin II. the Chalukya [*Ep. Ind.* vi. p. 10 and *Ind. Ant.* xiii. 70] ; but later he had to transfer his allegiance to the suzerain of the north, with whom he further allied himself by marrying his daughter. Orissa also formed a part of his empire [*Life of Hiuen Tsang*, p. 154]. Opinions differ as to his conquest of Nepal; for which the principal evidence relied upon is an era mentioned in the Nepalese inscriptions of the times, which, without any violence to chronology, may be taken as the era of Harṣa, indicating his overlordship of Nepal. The course of his conquests thus ran smooth in all directions till it was checked at the Vindhyas and the Revā by the southern sovereign Pulikeśin II., from whose suzerainty he had weaned away Valabhi [see Fleet's *Dynasties of the Kanarese Districts*, p. 350 f.]. It is stated in some inscriptions that "by his defeat of Śrī Harṣavardhana, the lord of entire northern India, Pulikeṣin won the title of Parameśvara" [*ib.*].

With the achievement of his suzerainty in the north Harṣa proceeded to put his army on a peace footing, that is, so to increase its force that it could make insubordination on the part of any of the states under his empire an absolute impossibility. His peace strength included as many as 60,000 elephants and 100,000 horse, as stated by the Chinese pilgrim. The elephants, according to Bāṇa (65), were acquired by the emperor as tribute or as presents or secured by the "rangers of his own elephant districts." The state elephant, the emperor's "friend in battle and sport," was called Darpaśāta, who "seemed to pour out again from his mouth the rivers he had drunk up in his triumphal progress of conquest"

(75). The king's horses came from many distant countries, "from Vanāyu (Arabia), Āraṭṭa, Kamboja, Bharadvāja, Sindh and Persia" (70). Harṣa's army also included troops of camels (66). With such a military force there is no wonder that he was able "to reign in peace for thirty years without raising a weapon," as Yuan Chwang states [Watters, ii. 343]. How his authority was felt even in the extremities of his empire is shown by one episode: the King of Assam was retaining as his guest the Chinese pilgrim whom Harṣa sent for, but the king sent the answer that Harṣa might have his head, but not his guest. "I trouble you for the head" came the immediate reply of Harṣa, which settled the matter. With peace and order thus enforced within his dominions, Harṣa, like Asoka, was free to devote himself to the pursuits of culture and learning, to engage in the solemn pomps and grand processions of religion instead of military displays and pageants. With the completion of his conquests he also turned towards Buddhism in accordance with his earlier resolve. He adopted Mahāyāna Buddhism under the teachings of Yuan Chwang, whom he first met in his camp at Kajugṛiha (Rajmahal) in Bengal [Watters ii. 183], although his ancestors were worshippers of the Tāntrika cult, of Śiva and the Sun [Bāṇa (109], (170); Sonpat Copper Seal inscription of Harṣa].

For the promotion of Mahāyāna Buddhism Harṣa convoked a grand religious assembly at Kanouj, to which were invited the exponents of the different Indian religions to listen to the discourse of Yuan Chwang. In his royal progress along the Ganges towards the Assembly the emperor was accompanied by his large retinue of soldiers and elephants, and by his friend, King Kumāra of Assam, with his own following of 20,000 elephants and 30,000 ships [*Life*, p. 172,] while at the assembly there were eighteen other kings together with 3000 Mahāyāna and Hīnayāna Buddhist monks, 3000 Brāhmans and Nirgranthas, and about 1000 Buddhist scholars from the Nālandā Monastery. There was seating accommodation for 2000 persons in two thatched halls, in which a golden image of Buddha was installed. Every day from the emperor's travelling palace the image of Buddha was carried in a procession of more than 300 elephants by the emperor and Kumāra, in the guise of Indra and Brahmā, and the other kings, and the chief officers, ministers and priests, and after offerings to the mage the proceedings began. Yuan Chwang had a placard hung outside the Assembly hall notifying that "he would offer his head to anyone who could find a single word of his contrary to reason." The Assembly went on smoothly for five days without any opposition, when the emperor, getting scent of a conspiracy against Yuan Chwang's life, proclaimed that anyone hurting the pilgrim would be beheaded, and, speaking against him, would have his tongue cut out. Upon this the opponents of Yuan Chwang left the Assembly in a body and, with freedom of discussion thus stifled, the Assembly went on smoothly for another eighteen days. Thus Yuan Chwang had no chance of offering his own head to any successful critic of his discouse! There, is, however, another version of the conspiracy, which makes it as against the king and not the pilgrim. It was a conspiracy of 500 Brāhmans, who, resenting the King's treatment of them at the Assembly, set fire to the tower of the Assembly hall and engaged an assassin to kill him. The foul design miscarried and the Brahman conspirators were deported to the frontiers of India.

He also served the cause of Buddhism in other ways. Once a year he summoned the Buddhist monks and entertained them for twenty-one days. He would also bring them together for discussion, and the best he would appoint and honour as his own teachers, while the morally deficient he would banish from his presence and country [Watters, I. 344]. He also endowed Buddhism with many buildings in different places. He forcibly secured from Kashmir the tooth-relic of the Buddha, which he enshrined in a monastery to the west of Kanouj. He made a gift of a temple of bronze, 100 feet in height, to the Nālandā monastery. Yuan Chwang says that he created thousands of topes, each about 100 feet high, on the banks of the Ganges and monasteries at the sacred places of Buddhism, while he also furnished the chapels and liberally adorned the common halls of the monasteries [*ib.*]. He also went much further than Asoka in forbidding under severe penalties the use of animal food throughout the Five Indies and the destruction of animal life.

As a consequence of his special attentions, his capital, the city of Kanouj, revived as a centre of Buddhism. While Fa-hien noticed only two monasteries there, Yuan Chwang could count there as many as 100.

With all his leanings towards Buddhism Harṣa was not hostile towards other faiths and communities, which were not excluded from the royal patronage. Every five years he used to hold an Assembly called the Assembly of Mokṣa, because "he gave away in religious alms everything except the material of war." One such Assembly was witnessed by Yuan Chwang, whom the emperor informed that it was the sixth in his reign [*Life*, p. 184]. The place fixed for it was Prayāga, as the holiest Hindu place, where 'it was more advantageous to give one mite in charity than a thousand in any other place" [*ib.*]. The "arena of charity" was the great sandy plain to the west of the confluence, to this day one of the sites of the Kumbha Melā, the most ancient, popular and crowded religious congress of India. Harṣa came to this Assembly from Kanouj, followed by twenty kings in his train, including King Kumāra of Assam, and his own son-in-law, Dhruvabhaṭṭa, King of Valabhai. They found a concourse of 500,000 people already gathered there. The first day saw the distribution of costly clothing and articles in worship of the Buddha; the next two days were given to the worship of the Sun and Śiva and charities halved in value as compared with the first day. On the fourth day 10,000 selected Buddhists were each given 100 pieces of gold, one pearl, one cotton garment, besides a variety of food and drink, flowers and perfumes. The next twenty days were occupied by gifts to the Brahmans, another ten days by gifts to the heretics, and another ten days to the seekers of alms from distant countries. The eighth distribution of charity was to the poor, the destitute and orhpans, taking a whole month. "By this time the accumulation of five years was exhausted. Except the horses, elephants and military accoutrements, which were necessary for maintaining order and protecting the royal estate, nothing remained. Besides these, the king freely gave away his gems and goods, his clothing and necklaces, and bright head-jewel,—all these he freely gave without stint. All being given away, he begged from his sister, Rājyaśrī, an ordinary second-hand garment, and, having put it on, he paid worship to the Buddhas of the ten regions," rejoicing that all his accumulated wealth and treasure were well bestowed [*ib*. p. 187]. It was thus a record in charity which no king in any age or clime can possibly beat. Yuan Chwang states that his daily charity comprised feeding 1000 Buddhists and 500 Brāhmans, even while on tour [Watters, i. 344].

His large-hearted liberality also expressed itself

in his manifold works of public utility. "In all the highways of the towns and villages throughout India, he erected hospices (*puṇyaśālās*) provided with food and drink, and stationed there physicians with medicines for travellers and poor persons round about, to be given without any stint" [Beal, i. 214]. The provision of medical aid at the Travellers' Rest-houses is an example even to present times! Bāṇa also is equally eloquent about Harṣa's public works and the humanity of his administration: "Beneath his rule the Golden Age seemed to bud forth in close packed lines of sacrificial posts, the evil time to flee in the smoke of sacrifices meandering over the sky, heaven to descend in stuccoed shrines, Dharma to blossom in white pennons waving over temple minarets, the villages to bring forth a progeny of beautiful arbours erected on their outskirts for meetings, alms houses, inns, and women's marquees" (133).

A religious and charitable man, Harṣa was also a great lover and patron of learning. Bāṇa describes how Harṣa excelled in poetical contests by his originality (79), how "his poetical skill found words fail and knowledge its subjects" (86). But the testimony of the courtier is supported by more impartial evidence. The Chinese traveller, I-tsing, who visited India (673-687 A.D.) after Harṣa's death, records how he was "exceedingly fond of literature." He used to call for poetical compositions by the literary men of his court, who at one time presented their sovereign with 500 poems dealing with the jātakas or previous births of the Buddha collected into the work called *Jātaka-mālā*. He himself also composed the play called *Nāgānanda* (based on "the story of the Bodhisattva Jīmūtavāhana surrendering himself in place of a Nāga"), which he had "set to music and performed by a band accompanied by dancing and acting" [I-tsing, ed. Takakusu, p. 163]. Historians of Sanskrit literature regard him as the author of two other dramas, the *Ratanāvalī* and *Priyadarśikā*, and also a grammatical work, while his fame as a poet leads Jayadeva, the author of the *Gītagovinda*, to rank him with Bāhsa and Kālidāsa. Among examples of his literary patronage, we know of Bāṇa himself, the author of the *Harṣa-charita* and *Kādambarī*, of Haridatta whom "he raised to eminence" [*Ep. Ind.*, i. 180], of Jayasena, a man of encyclopaedic learning, whom he offered to settle in Orissa by a gift of the revenue of eighty large towns there [*Life*, p. 154], and of Yuan Chwang, whom he throughout treated almost with royal honours. At the conclusion of the assembly at Kanouj the emperor offered him 10,000 pieces of gold, 30,000 pieces of silver, 100 garments of superior cotton, while the attending eighteen kings proposed each to give him rare jewels. But all this offer the Chinese pilgrim could not see his way as a truly spiritual man to accept [*Life*, p. 180]. Indeed, the rule of Harṣa's literary and religious patronage was that a fourth of the revenue from the crown lands was to be given away in rewarding high intellectual eminence, and another fourth in helping the various sects [Watters, i. 176].

These pursuits of peace, of culture and religion, imply the efficiency of his administration, for which, however, full details are not available. The supreme factor in that efficiency was the sovereign himself. By his campaigns and travels he made himself acquainted with every part of his vast empire from Kashmir and the Hūṇa country in the north to the Vindhyas and the Revā in the south, and from Orissa in the east to Valabhī in the west. Thus he acquired the first qualification of a ruler. Yuan Chwang says: "The king made visits of inspection throughout his dominions, not residing long at any place, but having temporary buildings erected for his residence at each place of sojourn; but he did not go abroad during the three months of the Rain-season retreat" [Watters, i. 344]. At the time of the Chinese pilgrim's visit, "the emperor was visiting different parts of his empire" [Beal, i. 215]. We can trace several places at which he camped out. Travelling as far as Kongyodha in the Ganjam district, he returned touring through Orissa [*Life*, pp. 159, 172] and was first seen by the Chinese pilgrim in his camp in Bengal at Kajugṛiha, Rajmahal. Next, we find him at Kanouj and Prāyaga in connexion with his assemblies, while Bāṇa saw him in his camp at Maṇitāra on the Ajiravatī (in Oudh).

He moved through his dominions in great state as befitted an emperor. Bāṇa describes (237) how, while he was on the march, "hired porters carried his golden footstools, water-pots, cups, spittoons and baths; his kitchen appurtenances with goats attached to thongs of pig-skin, a tangle of hanging sparrows and forequarters of venison, a collection of young rabbits, pot herbs and bamboo shoots, buttermilk pots, baskets containing a chaos of fire-trays, ovens, simmering pans spits, copper sauce-pans and frying pans," "while villagers awaited the touring king with presents of curds, molasses, candied sugar and flowers. The royal progresses were rendered more stately by the presence of the subordinate kings. Bāṇa describes how the royal camp at Maṇitāra was surrounded by "the many camps of the renowned subject-kings" and "filled on every side with conquered hostile vassal-chiefs," other kings who came to see his glory, ambassadors from every foreign country, and natives of every land, who could with great difficulty obtain an audience or sight of the emperor. In obtaining the interview granted to him Bāṇa had to "pass through three courts crowded with subject-kings," and in the fourth he saw King Harṣa in an open space in front of a pavilion with armed attendants in a line at a distance, favourites seated near him, and himself seated on a throne of stone shining like pearl, sporting with his subject-kings (78), his left foot placed on a footstool of sapphire girt round with a row of rubies (81). The jewelled footstool is also mentioned by Yuan Chwang. The exterior of the camp was marked by equal magnificance. The gate was dark with crowds of elephants; horses at another place, leaping up to the sky, made it appear "all in waves"; another place appeared tawny with troops of camels and another white with umbrellas or waving with moving chowries.

With all this pomp and luxury the emperor was the busiest of men. "The day was too short for him," says the Chinese pilgrim [Watters, i. 344]; "it was divided into three periods, of which one was given up to affairs of government, and two to religious works. He was indefatigable and forgot sleep and food in his devotion to good works."

Next, there seems to have been a Council of Ministers. Mantri-pariṣad, in the administration. They seem to have wielded real power on occasions. During the interregnum following the unexpected death of Rājyavardhana they elected Harṣa as king [Beal, i. 211]. They also decided that Rājyavardhana should attend the conference at the treacherous invitation of King Śaśāṅka and were thus responsible for his death [*ib.*]. The Chinese pilgrim also observes that "a commission of officers hold the land" [Beal, i. 210] (though it might refer to the system of paying the salaries of officers by grants of land).

We know of several ministers and officers of Harṣa by name. Bhaṇḍi was a chief minister who accompanied Rājyavardhana in his campaign against Mālwa—as stated by Bāṇa, though Yuan Chwang makes him the mover of the proposal by which the throne was offered to Harṣa on the death of Rājyavardhana. Avanti, according to Bāṇa, was "the supreme minister of war and peace," Siṃhanāda, the old commander-in-chief, and Skandagupta, the commandant of the elephant force (220).

The officers, according to Yuan Chwang, received their salaries in kind, in grants of land, and were paid according to their work. But soldiers were paid in cash and were enrolled on the basis of the summons and rewards announced. A fourth of the crown lands was absorbed by "the endowment of great public servants," while another fourth by "the expenses of government and state worship" [Watters, i. 176]. There was forced labour when the public works required it, but it was paid for [Beal, i. 87].

The Chinese pilgrim further tells us that "the government is honestly administered, the criminal class is small, the people live together on good terms, are of pure moral principles, do not practise deceit, keep their obligations, do not take anything wrongfully and yield more than fairness requires."

The Penal Code was, however, severe. Treason against the king was punished by life-long imprisonment. "For offences against social morality, and disloyal and unfilial conduct, the punishment is either mutilation of limbs or deportation of the offender to another country or into the wilderness. Other offences can be atoned for by a money payment." Trial by ordeal was also in vogue [Watters, i. 171-172].

The government was also "generous." "Official requirements are few; families are not registered; in the absence of forced labour everyone keeps to his hereditary occupation and attends to his patrimony." There were no large demands upon the liberties or the resources of the people. "Taxation was light." A sixth of the crops was the land revenue, while "light duties were levied at ferries and barrier stations" [Watters, i. 172-176].

The enlightened character of the administration is shown in the creation of a Department of Records and Archives. Both good and bad were faithfully recorded "in the official annals and state papers," while "instances of public calamity and good fortune are set forth in detail" [*ib.* 154]. One of the Harṣa inscriptions [*Ep. Ind.* i. 73], as well as Bāṇa (227), mentions the officers called *Mahākṣapaṭalika*, notary-in-chief, *Akṣapaṭalika*, the village notary, and the *Karaṇi* or clerk.

Although the details of Harṣa's administration are not fully known, we have a fair account in the pages of Yuan Chwang's *Travels* of the effects of the administration on the people and the country, of their material and moral progress. We shall consider the moral progress first.

The very visit of the Chinese pilgrim, and, indeed, of so many students from China and other countries in search of the saving knowledge which India during centuries could give, is itself the best proof of her moral progress and greatness. The empire of Indian thought extended far beyond the borders of India. Brāhamanism was its most important product. According to Yuan Chwang, India itself was then known to foreigners as "the country of the Brāhmans." He refers to Sanskrit as the language of the cultured classes including the Buddhists, the best Sanskrit, both spoken and written, being that of Mid-India, or Harṣa's empire, while outside Mid-India, there were variations from the original source and standard, which by use became the norm and gave rise to vulgar dialects removed from the pure style [Watters, i. 153]. Besides the language, Brāhmanism showed its vitality and vigour in the numerous ascetic sects and schools of philosophy such as the Bhūtas (covering themselves with ashes), the Nirgranthas (quite naked), the Kāpālikas (wearing necklace of skulls), the Jūṭikas (with matted hair) [*Life*, p. 161], worshippers of Durgā [*Ib.* p. 87], ascetics wearing peacocks' tails or pulling out their hair [Watters, i. 148], Digambaras, Pāśupatas [*ib.* 123], Sāṅkhyas and Vaiśeṣikas [*Life*, p. 161]. Bāṇa also in one passage mentions among the schools of philosophy of the times, the followers of Kapila, Kaṇāda, the Nyāya and Upaniṣads, the Lokāyatikas (materialists), followers of Kṛiṣṇa, ascetics who pulled out their hair (254 f.), and, in another passage (48) mentions ascetic widows, Pārāśara mendicants, Jain monks and Śaiva devotees.

The Chinese pilgrim also noticed the inner greatness of these Indian ascetics along with their external distinguishing marks. They all renounced the world and some of them a life of affluence in favour of a whole-hearted quest of Truth, depending for livelihood upon beggary and chance. "With them there is honour in knowing truth and no disgrace in being destitute. They are not moved by praise or blame (conquering the last infirmity of noble minds). The rulers treating them with ceremony and respect cannot make them come to court" (showing a thorough-going non-cooperation with the world, the devil and the flesh !). By their moral pre-eminence they commanded the esteem of both the king and the people. They did not, however, confine their knowledge and worth to themselves but tried to share them with their fellows in society. Yuan Chwang states that they knew not fatigue in teaching and travelling over long distances for its purposes [Watters, i. 161]. They were the real educators of thought, who did more to spread education and enlightenment in the country than any paid or official agency. The people found their own teachers irrespective of the state.

Buddhism was then showing signs of decline as compared with Brāhmanism. Besides its broad division into Mahāyāna and Hīnayāna, it was further split up into eighteen different sects with their own special literature cultivated in the monasteries owned by them. Some of these monasteries were very famous as seats of learning, where Yuan Chwang used to halt in his tour for instruction under their distinguished teachers. Thus in Kashmir he spent two years upon the study of some sūtras and śāstras and getting MSS. copied out. In the Nagaradhana Vihāra in Jālandhara he sought instruction from Chandravarmā. Jayagupta taught him in a monastery of the Śrughna country, which was such a famous seat of learning that "distinguished monks from other lands came there to have their doubts solved." A monastery at Matipura was known for its learned scholar Mitrasena, under whom Yuan Chwang studied for several months. In Kanouj was the Bhadra-Vihāra, where he studied for some time under the teacher, Vīryasena. The Tiloshika monastery near Nālandā was then "the rendezvous of eminent scholars, who flocked to it from all regions." At Gayā the Mahābodhi monastery had 1000 ecclesiastics, known for their Vinaya observances. At Monghyr were two teachers, Tathāgatagupta and Kṣāntisiṃha, under whom the pilgrim studied for a year. A monastery in Puṇyavardhana attracted students from East India, while the Raktamṛīttikā monastery in Karṇasuvarṇa was the resort of illustrious monks. All these monasteries mostly within the empire of Harṣa were singled out by Yuan Chwang as seats of Buddhist learning where he could profitably stay for study. But the most noted of them all was the monastery of Nālandā, in which was centred the Indian learning of the age.

Nālandā, in its six-storied monasteries, the gift of six kings, accommodated no less than 10,000 students, some from foreign countries like China and Mongolia [Takakusu's I-tsing, p. 26 and

Watters, ii. 165], for whom it provided, besides free lodging, free board, clothes, bedding, medicines and tuition, out of its endowment of the revenues of 100 villages granted by "a king of the country." The University, however, comprised only "Schools of Discussion" among the different sects and systems in the country, and was thus meant only for advanced scholars. The answer of difficult problems was the test for admission, which "only two or three out of ten could secure." Thus the 10,000 students of Nālandā were all advanced scholars, of whom 1510 were teachers giving 100 different discourses every day. "Learning and discussing, they found the day too short ; day and night they admonished each other, juniors and seniors mutually helping to perfection." Some of the more famous teachers at Nālandā are named : Guṇamati, Sthiramati, Jinamitra, Jñānachandra, Chandrapāla, Dharmapāla, the predecessor of Śīlabhadra, "by far the most learned man of the times" and the then head of the convent. Nālandā offered a wide range of studies connected with the various schools of Buddhism and even with Brāhmanical learning and secular subjects. They included the three Vedas, the Atharvaveda, Hetuvidyā (logic), Śabdavidyā (grammar and philology), Chikitsāvidyā (medicine), Sāṅkhya, Nyāya, Yoga-Śāstra and other subjects like law, philosophy, philology, astronomy and the grammar of Pāṇini. Yuan Chwang studied at Nālandā for five years, during which he mastered "all the collections of Buddhist books as well as the sacred book of the Brāhmans" [*Life*, pp. 112, 121, 125]. Thus Nālandā was a true University in the universality of its studies, in its ideal of freedom in learning, welcoming knowledge from all quarters, from all sects and systems, and, lastly, in its pedagogic method, the method of discussion for higher learning. Yuan Chwang gives an account of how this method worked in education. Once under instructions from his teacher, Śilabhadra, he was delivering a discourse at the University on the Yoga-Śāstra while a contrary discourse was being given in another part of the University by Siṃharaśmi. Yuan Chwang had at once to face him and silenced him by his arguments. His opponent, in shame, went to the Bodhi monastary at Gayā and brought thence a famous scholar of eastern India, Chandrasiṃha by name, who, however, could not prevail against Yuan Chwang. A Lokāyata Brāhman philosopher, writing out forty theses, hung them up at the gate of Nālandā with the following challenge : "If anyone within can refute these principles, I will then give my head as a proof of his victory." Yuan Chwang accepted the challenge, had the poster removed, and in the presence of the chancellor Śīlabhadra and all the students, by his discourse defeated his opponent, who remained to be his disciple and was spared his head [*Life*, pp. 157-164]. The Brāhman then went to Kumāra, King of Kāmarūpa, and reported to him about the learning of the pilgrim, which made the king send for him at once, as already narrated [*ib.*].

A picture of the same liberty and liberality in learning in that age is also given by Bāṇa in connexion with the hermitage of the Buddhist Saint, Divākaramitra, in the Vindhyan forests, who admitted as his disciples followers of every sect and school of thought, Buddhists from various provinces, Jains, Brāhman ascetics, Vaiṣṇavas, Brahmachārins, followers[1] of Kapila, Kaṇāda, Nyāya, Lokāyata, Upanisads, students of Smṛitis and Purāṇas, adepts in sacrifice, adepts in grammar, assayers of metals—"all diligently following their own tenets, pondering, urging objections, raising doubts, resolving them, giving etymologies, disputing, studying, and explaining." This was a typical Indian University of the times!

The learning and culture of the age were thus centred in these schools and monasteries, of which the Chinese pilgrim noticed as many as 5000 in the whole of India, accommodating for instruction over two lacs of monks belonging to different schools of Buddhism. That India could produce such a large number of people to sacrifice everything material and secular in the quest of the Ideal and Spiritual demonstrates the high level of moral progress attained by her in a particular direction.

We shall now consider the material progress of the country under Harṣa. Its highest level was, of course, seen in his capital and his palace. Kanouj now supplanted Pāṭaliputra as the premier city of northern India, "with its extension of 5 miles, its strong defences, its lofty structures, beautiful gardens and tanks, its museum of rarities collected from strange lands ; the refined appearance of its citizens, their clothes of glossy silk, their devotion to learning and arts, their clear and suggestive discourses and the number of the well-to-do classes and families of great wealth" [Watters, i. 340]. The earlier capital under his father was Sthāṇviśvara, which has been described by Bāṇa together with the palace. It resounded with the sounds of triumph, booming of drums, songs of troubadours and ministrels and bustle of business (170). Its principal street was the bazaar street (171). The palace had a street wall which was whitewashed (158). We read of its stairs (171) and the prince descending from the palace (179). It had four courts (171), which were large enough to look like "seas of elephants and horses" brought together on festive occasions (158). We read of its "mosaic floors of red lead" and decorations with the painting of auspicious scenes and modelling of clay figures of fishes, tortoises, crocodiles, cocoanuts, plantains and betel-trees. It was fitted with "crocodile-mouthed conduits which conveying scented water filled a variety of pleasure-ponds" (158). We also read of lions in their cages in the palace grounds, upon which Harṣa's mother wished to feast her eyes in the sickness of pregnancy ; of varieties of apes and orang-outangs, rare birds and mermen with necks bound in golden fetters ; "musk deer scenting the space all round them with their perfume ; female chamara deer parrots, śārikās and other birds enclosed in gold-painted bamboo cages and chattering copious wit, patridges in cages of coral," which were some of the presents sent by the King of Assam to Harṣa (245). Harṣa himself lived in great luxury. He bathed in vessels of gold and silver. His dress comprised a snow-white lower garment radiant with shot silk threads, a bejewelled girdle and a thin upper garment spangled with worked stars (80). He wore a necklace of pearls and other ornaments, which made him look "like a jewel mountain with its outstretched wings of jewels spread on both sides."

We shall now study the material progress as seen in the country at large. Cities were enclosed in quadrangular walls broad and high and generally built of bricks. Yuan Chwang considers the architecture of the Buddhist monasteries as "most remarkable." "They have a tower at each of the four corners of the quadrangle and three high halls in a tier. The rafters and roof beams are carved with strange figures and the doors, windows and walls are painted in various colours." The best example of this architecture was the Nālandā monastery. Yuan Chwang speaks of its storeyed buildings, richly adorned towers, upper rooms and turrets towering above the clouds. The massive external grandeur of the buildings contrasted with the delicate beauty of their interior with the "dragon-like projections, coloured eaves, pearl-red pillars carved

and ornamented, richly adorned balustrades and roofs covered with shining tiles reflecting light in a thousand shades" while "the sculpture was perfect" [*Life*, p. 111, and Watters, ii. 165]. The private houses had "a sumptuous inside but a simple outside," with "their halls and terraced belvederes, which had wooden flat-roofed rooms" and were "of great height." The poor men's houses were "of brick or board and thatched with grass, with their walls ornamented with chunam and floor purified with cow-dung and strewn with flowers of the season." There were seats of corded benches, of which the frames were variously carved and adorned according to the tastes and resources of the owners.

There was some kind of town planning too. Shops were placed on the highways, not very broad ones, according to Yuan Chwang, and the booths or inns on the roads. Persons following unclean or disreputable occupations had to live outside the city. These were butchers, executioners, scavengers, fishermen and public performers, whose abodes were also marked out by distinguishing signs.

The material development of the country was also reflected in the various articles of consumption. The clothing of the people was of various kinds. Yuan Chwang noticed the *Kauśeya* cloths (of silk and cotton), the *Kṣauma* (made of fabrics from the stuffs yielded by the flax, the jute and the hemp plants), the *Kambala* (of wool or blanket) and a fourth variety also of wool of a particularly fine character. The style of dress was simple. It comprised an inner and outer clothing needing no tailoring work. "The men wind a strip of cloth round the waist and up to the armpits and leave the shoulder bare. The women wear a long robe which covers both shoulders and falls down loose". In parts of northern India close-fitting jackets were used in winter. Yuan Chwang had a fur-lined cape from the King of Assam to protect him from cold on his return journey by the land route to China. Ornaments were widely used by kings and grandees. Garlands and jewelled tiaras were used for the head and rings, bracelets, and necklaces for the body. Wealthy merchants used only bracelets.

Industrial life was organised on the basis of castes and of larger corporations than castes, the guilds. The Brahmans had no part in the industrial activities of the country, but lived like non-economic men for spiritual ends. The Kṣatriyas carried on the administration, and the Vaiśyas trade, inland and foreign. Agriculture was for the Śūdras. Thus caste determined the craft. Yuan Chwang refers to "mixed castes," *i.e.* corporations admitting of a heterogenous composition, and hence guilds, which were numerous in the country [Watters, i. 147, 148, 168]. Bāṇa also describes how on the occasion of the marriage of Princess Rājyaśrī, "from every country were summoned guilds of skilled artists" to decorate

the palace, such as carpenters, painters, modellers and the like (158).

The money in India included not merely gold and si'ver coins, but also cowries and small pearls [Watters, i. 178].

Yuan Chwang also gives us a glimpse of the social conditions of the times. The first two castes were known for their purity and simple habits. There were no marriages between different castes or between relations on the father's or mother's side. The Indians as a people were known for their physical purity. "Before every meal they must have a wash. The fragments and remains of food are not served up again nor are the food utensils passed on. The utensils of pottery and wood were thrown away if once used in eating, but those of gold, silver, copper or iron were cleansed for fresh use." The Indians also observed purity in diet. "Onions and garlic are little used, and people who eat them are ostracised." Meat was forbidden food, except mutton and vension. Fish was allowed as food, but the common diet comprised milk, ghee, granulated sugar, sugar-candy, cakes and parched grain with mustard oil [*ib.* 140, 151, 152, 168 and 178].

The women of the upper classes went in for education. Princess Rājyaśrī received her instruction in Buddhist doctrines from the sage Divākaramitra, whom her royal brother appointed for the purpose, as stated by Bāṇa (289). She was thus educated enough to appreciate the discourse of Yuan

Chwang on Mahāyāna doctrines, to which she listened while "sitting behind the king" [*Life*, p. 176]. Thus she did not observe the *purdah*. This is also apparent from her free wanderings among the Vindhyan hills in her earlier life, as also from her presence at the assembly of Prayāga [*ib*. p. 187]. From her case we may also infer that girls were married very early, before puberty, while there was no second marriage for a woman, as stated by Yuan Chwang. The custom of *Satī* was then prevalent. Queen Yaśovatī died as a Satī before her husband's death, as already narrated, while Princess Rājyaśrī herself was only just rescued from the same fate.

Sea-voyages for commercial and political purposes were common. A Brāhman was sent by Harṣa as envoy to China in 641 A.D. When commencing his return journey to China, Yuan Chwang was thus addressed by Harṣa : "If you select the southern sea-route, then I will send official attendants to accompany you." Thus the sea-route to China was then quite familiar. It was taken by Fa-hien in the fourth century and by I-tsing in the seventh. Both have indicated the several intermediate stations along that route. Fa-hien sailed from Tāmralipti to Ceylon in fourteen days, whence he came to Java, and from there, by a voyage of fifty days his boat, carrying 200 passengers was expected to arrive at Kwang-chow on the Chinese coast. The stages in I-tsing's voyage were : (1) Bhoja, twenty days' sail from China ; (2) "The country of the Naked

People" on the Atchin coast, about ten days' sail from Ka-cha, a port of embarkation in the country of Śri-Bhoja ; (3) Tāmralipti, about a fortnight's voyage. Regarding the return journey he gives the following particulars : (1) From Tāmralipti to Ka-cha, a voyage of two months ; (2) from Ka-cha to Bhoja, another month's voyage ; (3) from Bhoja to Kwang-fu, about a month's voyage more. The age of Harṣa was one of extensive emigrations from India, which colonised Java. The emigrations were from the western, Gujarat coast of India and are believed to have been caused by political unrest in the country, The immigrants must have been the Śaka, who were displaced by the conquests of Chandragupta II., and the White Huns by the conquests of the Sassanians and Turks (A.D. 500-600), which intercepted their retreat northwards. Upon these came the further conquests of King Prabhākaravardhana in the countries of the Huns, the Gurjaras, the Lāṭas of Gandhāra, Sindh and Malwa and those of the Emperor Harṣa himself. Thus swarms of refugees were seeking the Gujarat ports for escape from a land of confusion into fresh fields and pastures new. Among them were the craftsmen to whom we owe the famous monuments of Borobudur and Prambanam in Java, the best examples of Indian art.

The genealogy of Harṣa is given in two inscriptions, one of the Banskhera plate and the other on the Sonpat cooper seal. It is thus given in both :

Mahārāja Naravardhana
m. Vajriṇīdevī
|
Mahārāja Rājyavardhana I.
m. Apsarodevī
|
Mahārāja Ādityavardhana
m. Mahāsenaguptādevī
|
Mahārajādhirāja Prabhākaravardhana
m. Yaśomatīdevī
|

Mahārajādhirāja Rājayavardhana II.	Mahārājādhirāja Harṣa	Rājyaśrī

According to Bāṇa (59) Harṣa had another brother named Kṛiṣṇa, and also a young son -(101). He had, of course, a daughter, who was married to Dhruvabhaṭṭa, King of Valabhī.

According to the *Life* (p. 156) Harṣa died "towards the end of the Yung Hui period," *i.e.* about 655 A.D., a date accepted by Takakusu [*I-tsing*, pp. lvi. and 163]. But Watters [i. 347] points out that according to Chinese history it should be 648 A.D., when the Chinese envoy to India found a usurper on the throne of Harṣa. He further states that Yuan Chwang submitted his Records to Tai Tsung in 648 A.D. and that he did so presumably after Harṣa's death.

At page,	in line,	read,	for
1	12	Hūṇa	Hum
3	28	Brāhman	Brāhaman
7	9	Brāhman	Brāhanan
8	19	latter	later
10	13	Brāhman	Brahaman
12	25	Deussen's	Dussen's
20	10	Oh	Of
21	29	Varcho	Carcho
22	10	at	in
29	2n	reading	reaching
41	6	thou	though
43	4	food	good
50	11n	Brāhmanical	Brāhamanica
53	14	Sañjaya	Sayñayya
54	24	respect	respects
57	2	books	book
57	10	ministry	ministy
62	8	test	tests
67	20	Mallas	Malas
67	25	owed	owned
68	12	Banaras	Benaras
71	3	lying	laying
74	29	witless	withless
82	10	trodden	troden
89	11	or	of
90	10	Brāhman	Brāhaman
96	19	Mānsēhrā	Mānsirā
97	2	inscribed	inscirbed
98	4	Bihār	Behār
100	15	dharma	darma
104	16	left	felt
108	17	Tusāspha	Tuṣāpha
111	20	Dharma	Dhamra
112	11	Pāṇḍyas	Pāṇḍayas
114	30	Sampratipatti	Samprdānatipatti
122	3n	Church	Chruch
122	9n	craved	carved

At page,	in line,	read,	for
127	14	relief of	relief
129	3	Buddha	Budha
131	9	literacy	litaracy
137	22	Garhwāl	Garwāl
138	25	Meghavarṇa	Meghavarman
139	7	storeys	stories
147	6	appears	apears
148	24	Vasubaṇdhu	Vasubahdhu
151	28	Grahavarman	Granavarman
152	8	had	has
153	11	and	an
153	15	Svarāstra	Savarāṣṭra
153	22	Valabhi	Valabhai
158	29	Valabhi	Valabhai
159	12	orphans	orhpans
161	14	Bhāsa	Bāhsa
171	16	monastery	monastary
179	14	Śakas	Saka